CANADIAN SOC   E

Top 100

WOMEN'S FOOTBALLERS

CANADIAN SOCCER'S ALL-TIME
TOP 100 WOMEN'S FOOTBALLERS

footballMedia / by Richard Scott
Copyright © 2023-2024 Up North Productions.
No reproduction without permission.
All rights reserved. April 2024.
ISBN 978-1-7383469-3-6

Published in Canada by:
Up North Productions
1995 Indian Creek Road
Limoges, ON   K0A 2M0
books@footballmedia.ca

Cover design by Griffin Scott. Christine Sinclair cover photo by Richard Scott.
All headshots courtesy and credit Canada Soccer.

CANADIAN SOCCER'S
TOP 100 WOMEN'S FOOTBALLERS

CANADIAN SOCCER'S ALL-TIME

PAGE / TOP 100 FOOTBALLERS		JERSEY & POSITION		CANADA "A" MP / G			
8	Agnew, Lindsay		22	RB	2017	2021	15	
9	Allen, Amber		19	M / F	2002	2008	25	6g
10	Andrews, Sasha		4	CB	2002	2010	47	3g
11	Beckie, Janine		16	F / FB	2014	(2023)	101	36
12	Bélanger, Josée		9	RB / F	2004	2017	57	7g
13	Booth, Melanie		3	LB	2002	2013	66	1g
14	Bowie, Mary Beth		18	M	1999	2002	13	
15	Boyd, Breanna		3	RB / CB	2000	2003	43	2g
16	Brand, Sue	H.O.F.	14	LB / CB	1987	1991	20	
17	Buchanan, Kadeisha		3	CB	2012	(2023)	140	4g
18	Burtini Gerela, Silvana	H.O.F.	17	F	1987	2003	77	38
19	Cant, Connie	H.O.F.	13	M	1986	1991	22	4g
20	Carle, Gabrielle		21	FB / M	2015	(2023)	38	1g
21	Caron, Annie	H.O.F.	11	M / W	1986	1995	34	8g
22	Chapman, Allysha		2	LB	2009	(2023)	99	2g
23	Chapman, Candace	H.O.F.	9	CB	2002	2012	114	6g
24	Chin Baker, Carla	H.O.F.	18	GK	1986	1997	29	
25	D'Angelo, Sabrina		18	GK	2010	(2023)	14	
26	David, Tracy	H.O.F.	5	RB / CB	1986	1989	7	
27	Dennis, Tanya		6	RB	2003	2007	18	
28	Dion, Marie-Claude		8	CB	1993	2001	27	
29	Donnelly, Geri	H.O.F.	6	M	1986	2000	71	9g
30	Filigno Hopkins, Jonelle		16	F	2008	2015	71	11
31	Fleming, Jessie		17	M	2013	(2023)	123	19
32	Franck, Tanya		4	FB / M	1997	2000	29	3g
33	Franko, Martina (née Holan)	H.O.F.	10	CB / F	2005	2009	55	5g
34	Gareau Rudolph, Fabienne		17	F	1987	1991	17	5g
35	Gayle, Robyn	H.O.F.	5	RB	2006	2015	81	2g
36	Gerrior Williams, Suzanne		19	M	1990	1995	10	
37	Gilles, Vanessa		14	CB	2019	(2023)	34	3g
38	Grosso, Julia		7	M	2017	(2023)	57	3g
39	Hafting de Boer, Jenny		7	RB / F	1988	1995	12	
40	Harvey, Isabelle		12	F / M	1998	2004	44	3g
41	Hawthorne, Wendy		1	GK	1988	1998	15	
42	Helland, Janine (née Wood)	H.O.F.	9	CB	1989	1999	47	1g
43	Hellstrom, Jenna		31	W / FB	2017	2023	6	
44	Hermus, Randee	H.O.F.	11	CB / M	1998	2008	113	12
45	Hooper, Charmaine	H.O.F.	10	F / CB	1986	2006	129	71
46	Huitema, Jordyn		9	F	2017	(2023)	73	18
47	Iacchelli, Selenia		18	M / F	2005	2015	4	
48	Joly, Dr. Sarah		14	CB / M	1996	2000	17	1g
49	Julien, Christina		15	F	2009	2015	54	10
50	Kelly, Angela	H.O.F.	13	M	1990	1995	29	1g
51	Kiss, Kristina		2	M / FB	2000	2008	75	8g
52	Kyle, Kaylyn		6	M	2008	2015	101	6g
53	Labbé, Stephanie		1	GK	2004	2022	86	
54	Lacasse, Cloé		20	F	2021	(2023)	28	3g
55	Lang Romero, Kara	H.O.F.	15	F / M	2002	2014	92	34
56	Latham, Christine		2	F	2000	2006	49	15
57	Lawrence, Ashley		10	FB / M	2012	(2023)	126	8g

PAGE / TOP 100 FOOTBALLERS	JERSEY & POSITION			CANADA "A" MP / G			
58	LeBlanc, Karina	H.O.F.	1	GK	1998	2015	110	
59	Lemieux, Janet	H.O.F.	7	CB	1986	1987	6	
60	Leon, Adriana		19	F / W	2011	(2023)	105	31
61	Maglio, Sara		8	F	1997	2000	5	
62	Matheson, Diana		8	M	2003	2020	206	19
63	McEachern, Joan	H.O.F.	12	M	1987	1995	31	2g
64	McLeod, Erin		1	GK	2002	2022	119	
65	Mongrain, Luce	H.O.F.	16	CB / RB	1987	1995	30	
66	Morneau, Isabelle	H.O.F.	7	LB	1995	2006	87	6g
67	Moscato, Carmelina	H.O.F.	4	CB / M	2002	2015	94	2g
68	Muir, Suzanne	H.O.F.	15	M / FB	1994	1999	31	2g
69	Nault, Marie-Eve		20	LB	2003	2017	71	
70	Neil, Andrea	H.O.F.	5	M / FB	1990	2007	132	24
71	Nonen, Sharolta		6	CB	1999	2006	63	1g
72	O'Brien, Veronica		10	M / FB	1990	1997	31	1g
73	Parker, Kelly		15	M	2001	2012	40	3g
74	Prince, Nichelle		15	W / F	2012	(2023)	96	16
75	Quinn		5	M / CB	2014	(2023)	96	6g
76	Ring Passant, Michelle	H.O.F.	4	CB / M	1986	1995	45	2g
77	Riviere, Jayde		8	RB	2017	(2023)	43	1g
78	Robinson, Jodi-Ann		10	F	2004	2013	56	7g
79	Rose, Deanne		6	W / F	2015	(2023)	77	11
80	Rosenow Tenney, Shannon		11	F	1996	2000	28	11
81	Ross, Cathy	H.O.F.	12	CB / RB	1986	1995	34	3g
82	Rustad, Dr. Clare		4	M / CB	2000	2009	45	3g
83	Saiko, Anita (née Brand)		6	M	1986	1986	-	
84	Schmidt, Sophie		13	M / CB	2005	(2023)	226	20
85	Scott, Desiree		11	M	2009	(2023)	185	
86	Serwetnyk, Carrie	H.O.F.	10	F	1986	1996	18	1g
87	Sesselmann, Lauren		10	LB / CB	2011	2015	46	
88	Sheridan, Kailen		1	GK	2016	(2023)	43	
89	Simon, Sue	H.O.F.	21	GK	1986	1987	4	
90	Sinclair, Christine		12	F	2000	(2023)	331	190
91	Smith Herbert, Liz		2	M	1996	2000	22	2g
92	Stewart, Chelsea		3	FB / M	2008	2014	44	
93	Stoumbos, Helen	H.O.F.	2	F	1993	1999	35	1g
94	Swiatek, Taryn		20	GK	2000	2007	24	
95	Tancredi, Dr. Melissa		14	F	2004	2017	125	27
96	Thorlakson, Katie		16	F	2004	2007	23	2g
97	Timko Baxter, Brittany	H.O.F.	17	F / FB	2002	2012	132	5g
98	Vamos, Lydia		15	F	1989	1994	24	7g
99	Vermeulen, Amy		19	M	2001	2009	12	1g
100	Viens, Evelyne		13	F	2012	(2023)	22	4g
101	Walsh, Amy	H.O.F.	13	M	1998	2009	102	5g
102	Walsh, Cindy		5	CB	1998	2010	24	
103	Wilkinson, Rhian	H.O.F.	7	RB / F	2003	2017	181	7g
104	Woeller, Shannon		20	CB	2009	2019	21	
105	Wright, Nicole		1	GK	1996	2002	37	
106	Zadorsky, Shelina		4	CB	2012	(2023)	95	4g
107	Zurrer, Emily		2	CB	2004	2015	82	3g

GOALKEEPER
1 • STEPHANIE LABBÉ
The world's best goalkeeper in 2020-21. Stopped penalty kicks to win an Olympic Gold Medal.

RIGHT BACK
7 • RHIAN WILKINSON
Terrific two-way player who could seemingly run all day. Began her career as a forward.

CENTRE BACK
3 • KADEISHA BUCHANAN
Canada's greatest centre back ever. She can calmly shut down opposing strikers.

CENTRE BACK
9 • CANDACE CHAPMAN
Smart, quick and strong centre back who was also at ease moving the play forward.

LEFT BACK
10 • ASHLEY LAWRENCE
World-class player who would make Canada's ultimate XI at right back, left back or midfield.

MIDFIELDER
11 • DESIREE SCOTT
An aggressive player who excels as Canada's defensive dynamo. Known as the Destroyer.

MIDFIELDER
8 • DIANA MATHESON
Canada's London 2012 hero from the Olympic Games. Tireless and excellent sparkplug at midfield.

MIDFIELDER
13 • SOPHIE SCHMIDT
Energetic midfielder with great passing skills who can attack or defend at both sides of the pitch.

MIDFIELDER
17 • JESSIE FLEMING
Superb attacking midfielder who has impressive playmaking skills and excellent vision.

FORWARD
10 • CHARMAINE HOOPER
Canada's super striker for more than 20 years. Played at centre back for her last FIFA World Cup.

FORWARD
12 • CHRISTINE SINCLAIR
Canada's Captain Everything. She is exceptional at scoring goals or setting up teammates.

SUB • MIDFIELDER
6 • GERI DONNELLY
Canada's first goalscorer and all-time leader in appearances, was part of Canada's "Marvelous Midfield."

SUB • ATTACKING MID
15 • KARA LANG
With a rocket shot, she co-led Canada in goals scored in 2003 when she was still a teenager.

SUB • MIDFIELDER / FB
5 • ANDREA NEIL
A physical, hard-working midfielder who was one of the game's most influential leaders.

SUB • FORWARD
14 • MELISSA TANCREDI
A fierce attacking forward who could combine brilliantly up front with her teammates.

SUB • MIDFIELDER / F
17 • BRITTANY TIMKO BAXTER
Adept at playing any position from fullback to forward. She will score goals when up front.

SUB • GOALKEEPER
1 • KARINA LeBLANC
Canada's first two-time Concacaf champion, she retired as Canada's all-time leader with 47 clean sheets.

SUB • GOALKEEPER
1 • ERIN McLEOD
Goalkeeping hero from the London 2012 Olympic Games and Canada's home FIFA World Cup in 2015

The Canada Soccer Hall of Fame honours greats of the game from more than 150 years of football in Canada. From 2000 to 2024, the Canada Soccer Hall of Fame has honoured its first 212 members who were either players, coaches/managers, referees or builders.

MODERN (WNT)
Sue Brand
Silvana Burtini Gerela
Connie Cant
Annie Caron
Candace Chapman
Carla Chin Baker
Tracy David
Geri Donnelly
Martina Franko
Robyn Gayle
Randee Hermus
Charmaine Hooper
Angela Kelly
Kara Lang
Karina LeBlanc
Janet Lemieux
Joan McEachern
Luce Mongrain
Isabelle Morneau
Carmelina Moscato
Suzanne Muir
Andrea Neil
Michelle Ring Passant
Cathy Ross
Carrie Serwetnyk
Sue Simon
Helen Stoumbos
Brittany Timko Baxter
Amy Walsh
Rhian Wilkinson
Janine Wood Helland

MODERN (MNT)
Patrice Bernier
Jim Brennan
Ian Bridge
Alex Bunbury
John Catliff
Carlo Corazzin
Nick Dasovic
Dwayne De Rosario
Jason deVos
Paul Dolan
Craig Forrest

Gerry Gray
Richard Hastings
Lyndon Hooper
John Limniatis
Kevin McKenna
Colin Miller
Dale Mitchell
• Domenic Mobilio
Terry Moore
Pat Onstad
Paul Peschisolido
Tomasz Radzinski
Randy Ragan
Randy Samuel
Branko Segota
Paul Stalteri
Mike Sweeney
Carl Valentine
Mark Watson
Frank Yallop

PAST (POST WW2)
• Frank Ambler
• Dick Arends
Garry Ayre
• Eddie Bak
• Jim Blundell
Bob Bolitho
Jack Brand
• Roy Cairns
• Marcel Castonguay
• Paul Castonguay
• Roland Castonguay
Tony Chursky
• Jack Cowan
• Errol Crossan
Jimmy Douglas
Neil Ellett
• Bill Gill
• Doug Greig
• Bob Harley
• Trevor Harvey
• Art Hughes
Robert Iarusci
• Gordon Ion

Glen Johnson
Victor Kodelja
Bob Lenarduzzi
Sam Lenarduzzi
Tino Lettieri
Carmine Marcantonio
• Don Matheson
John McGrane
Normie McLeod
Wes McLeod
• Doug McMahon
• Bobby Newbold
Les Buzz Parsons
• Ken Pears
• Brian Philley
• Pat Philley
• Harry Phillips
Brian Robinson
John Schepers
Bobby Smith
• Jimmy Spencer
• Andy Stevens
Gary Stevens
• Gogie Stewart
• Mike Stojanović
David Stothard
Gene Vazzoler
• Jackie Whent
• Fred Whittaker
Bruce Wilson
• NIR/Jimmy Nicholl

PAST (PRE WW2)
• George Anderson
• Walter Bowman
• Geordie Campbell
• Joe Clulow
• Jock Coulter
• Eddie Derby
• Fred Dierden
• Ernie Edmunds
• Bill Findler
• Pete Larry Fitzpatrick
• George Graham
• Art Halliwell

• Bobby Lavery
• Eddie MacLaine
• Harry Manson
• Bill Matthews
• Jimmy Moir
• Jimmy Nelson
• Alec Smith
• Dickie Stobbart
• Tiny Thombs
• Dr. Walter Thomson
• Dave Turner
• Stan Wakelyn
• Artie Woutersz
• ENG/Sam Chedgzoy
• SCO/Joe Kennaway
• NIR/Whitey McDonald

BUILDER
• George Anderson
• Arthur Arnold
Brian Avey
Angus Barrett
• Herb Capozzi
• Jeff Cross
• Sam Davidson
• Sam Donaghey
• Gus Etchegarry
• Billy Fenton
• Jim Fleming
• David Forsyth
• Dr. Tom Fried
• Dave Fryatt
Bill Gilhespy
• Dr. Rudy Gittens
• George Gross
• Bill Hoyle
• Jim Hubay
• Alex Hylan
Colin Jose
• Johnny Kerr
• Eric King
• Graham Leggat
• John McMahon
• Lou Moro
Kevin Muldoon

Christine O'Connor
• Len Peto
Pat Quinn
• Terry Quinn
• John Richardson
• Tom Robertson
• John Russell
• Aubrey Sanford
Bob Sayer
Georges Schwartz
• Bill Simpson
Leeta Sokalski
• Alan Southard
• Dr. Fred Stambrook
• Steve Stavro
• Bill Stirling
Les Wilson
Derek Wisdom

COACH-MANAGER
• Jimmie Adam
• Bob Bearpark
Sylvie Béliveau
Chris Bennett
Stuart Brown
• John Buchanan
Bert Goldberger
Dick Howard
• Don Petrie
• Ted Slade
• Bill Thomson
Bruce Twamley
• Tony Waiters

REFEREE
Gord Arrowsmith
Sonia Denoncourt
Tony Evangelista
• Dan Kulai
• Horace Lyons
• Ray Morgan
Bob Sawtell
• Dino Soupliotis
Héctor Vergara
Werner Winsemann

RIGHT BACK

LINDSAY AGNEW

Born: 1995-03-31, Kingston, ON, CAN. Grew up in Kingston, ON, CAN & Dublin, OH, USA. Height 174 cm. Dominant right foot.

1 FIFA World Cup: Round of 16 at France 2019
1 Concacaf medal: Silver in 2018
1st #CANWNT: 2017-03-06 at São João da Venda, POR (v. POR)

INTERNATIONAL CAREER

Lindsay Agnew represented Canada at two FIFA youth tournaments and one FIFA World Cup. She also won a Concacaf Silver Medal at the 2018 Concacaf Championship when Canada qualified for the FIFA World Cup.

She made her international debut at the 2017 Algarve Cup and featured in the Final when Canada lost 1-0 to Spain. She also featured in the Algarve Cup in 2018 and 2019.

From 2017 to 2021, Agnew made 15 career international appearances with Canada.

On 24 February 2021, she made her last appearance at the SheBelieves Cup. She featured as a substitute in the second half in a 2-0 loss to Brazil.

CLUB CAREER

Agnew played her club football in Canada, USA, Australia and Sweden. From 2017 to 2021 across two stints in the NWSL, Agnew played for the Washington Spirit, Houston Dash and North Carolina Courage. In between those two stints, she spent the 2020 season with KIF Örebro in Sweden's Damallsvenskan.

Agnew played her college soccer at Ohio State University where she was a Second Team All-Big Ten selection in 2016. Growing up, she played her youth football in Ontario, New York and Ohio.

CANADA RECORDS

"A" RECORDS	MP	MS	MIN	G	A
2017 CANADA	7	2	336		
2018 CANADA	3	2	162		
2019 CANADA	4	1	134		
2021 CANADA	1	0	32		
4 SEASONS	15	5	664		

FIFA / OLYMPIC	MP	MS	MIN	G	A
2019 FIFA WC	0	0	0		

● ● ●

2019 FIFA WORLD CUP • Lindsay Agnew represented Canada at the 2019 FIFA Women's World Cup in France when they reached the Round of 16. In October 2018, she made two appearances at the Concacaf Championship when Canada qualified for France 2019 and reached the Concacaf Final in Texas.

AMBER ALLEN

MIDFIELDER / F

Born: 1975-10-21, Chilliwack, BC, CAN. Grew up in Pitt Meadows, BC, CAN. Height 173 cm. Dominant left foot.

Missed FIFA World Cups in 2003 and 2007 through injury
Missed Olympic Games in 2008 through injury
1st #CANWNT: 2002-03-01 at Quarteira, POR (v. SCO)
1st Goal: 2002-03-05 FWCQ at Silves, POR (v. POR)

INTERNATIONAL CAREER

Amber Allen represented Canada 25 times at the international "A" level, but missed the opportunity to feature at major tournaments from 2003 to 2008.

Allen missed back-to-back FIFA World Cups as well as an Olympic Games through injuries.

In 2003, she missed the FIFA World Cup after suffering a right knee injury and then a broken left leg. Four years later, she missed the FIFA World Cup after suffering another broken left leg.

In 2008, she was named to Canada's roster for the Olympic Games in Beijing, but she had to pull out because of her recurring leg injury. She played her last international match on 26 July 2008, just 11 days before Canada's Olympic opener in Tianjin, China.

CLUB CAREER

She played with Vancouver Whitecaps FC and won the USL W-League Championship twice in a three-year run (2004, 2006). She was a two-time All-Western Team all-star and a 2004 Championship All-Tournament Team all-star. She scored a career-high 17 goals in 14 matches in 2005. Six of those goals came in the playoffs when Vancouver finished in third place.

Allen played her college soccer at McGill University in Montréal. She was a CIAU First Team All-Canadian in 2000.

CANADA RECORDS

"A" RECORDS	MP	MS	MIN	G	A
2002 CANADA	5	3	218	2g	
2003 CANADA	6	1	148	1g	
2005 CANADA	6	1	153	1g	
2006 CANADA	0	0	0		
2007 CANADA	3	2	215	2g	
2008 CANADA	5	3	139		
6 SEASONS	**25**	**10**	**873**	**6g**	

FIFA / OLYMPIC	MP	MS	MIN	G	A
2003 FIFA WC	INJ	-	-		
2007 FIFA WC	INJ	-	-		
2008 OLYMPIC	INJ	-	-		

1st INTERNATIONAL GOAL • Amber Allen scored her first international goal in her third match when Canada beat the hosts Portugal at the 2002 Algarve Cup. Canada won 7-1 after Allen scored the opener. One month later, Allen scored her second international goal in a 3-2 loss to Japan at a tournament in Limoges, France.

CENTRE BACK

SASHA ANDREWS

Born: 1983-02-14, Edmonton, AB, CAN. Height 180 cm. Dominant right foot.

1 FIFA World Cup: 4th Place at USA 2003
2 Concacaf medals: Silver in 2002 and 2006
1st #CANWNT: 2002-03-01 at Quarteira, POR (v. SCO)
1st Goal: 2003-08-31 at Edmonton, AB, CAN (v. MEX)

INTERNATIONAL CAREER

Sasha Andrews represented Canada at one FIFA youth tournament and one FIFA World Cup. She also won a Bronze Medal at the Pan American Games in 2007.

At the FIFA U-19 World Championship in 2002, she scored the winning kick in the Semifinals that sent Canada through to the Final. Canada lost the Final three days later to USA on a golden goal.

In 2003, Andrews helped Canada set a program record with a 10-match undefeated streak before the FIFA World Cup.

In all, Andrews made 47 international "A" appearances for Canada from 2002 to 2010. She was just 19 years old when she made her debut at the 2002 Algarve Cup against Scotland. In 2009, she made her last appearance in the Cyprus Cup Final.

CLUB CAREER

Andrews has played her club football in Canada, USA, Norway, Australia and Iceland. She won the USL W-League Championship with both Vancouver Whitecaps FC (2004, 2006) and California's Pali Blues (2008, 2013). She also reached the Final in 2011. She won USL W-League Defender of the Year honours in 2004.

Andrews played her college soccer at the University of Nebraska. At the youth level, she won Canada Soccer's U-17 Cup with Edmonton Mill Woods SC in 2000.

CANADA RECORDS

"A" RECORDS	MP	MS	MIN	G	A
2002 CANADA	6	5	470		
2003 CANADA	15	6	665	2g	
2004 CANADA	1	0	7		
2005 CANADA	8	6	519	1g	
2006 CANADA	9	2	218		
2007 CANADA	5	0	109		
2009 CANADA	3	2	225		
2010 CANADA	0	0	0		
8 SEASONS	47	21	2213	3g	

FIFA / OLYMPIC	MP	MS	MIN	G	A
2003 FIFA WC	2	1	91		

● ● ●

2003 FIFA WORLD CUP • Sasha Andrews made two appearances at the FIFA Women's World Cup USA 2003 when Canada finished in fourth place. Andrews featured as a late substitute in the group phase victory over Argentina (a 3-0 win in Columbus) and then started the Match for Third Place against USA (a 3-1 loss in Carson, California).

16

JANINE BECKIE

WINGER / FB

Born: 1994-08-20, Littleton, CO, USA. Grew up in Highlands Ranch, CO, USA. Height 172 cm. Dominant right foot.

1 FIFA World Cup: Round of 16 at France 2019
2 Olympic Games: Bronze at Rio 2016, Gold at Tokyo in 2021
4 Concacaf medals: Silver in 2016, 2018, 2020, 2022
1st #CANWNT: 2014-11-26 at Los Angeles, CA, USA (v. SWE)
1st Goal: 2015-01-11 at Shenzhen, CHN (v. KOR)

OLYMPIC CHAMPION

Janine Beckie has already represented Canada at one FIFA youth tournament, one FIFA World Cup and two Olympic Games. She led Canada in goals in 2016 and 2017 and she led Canada in assists in 2021.

She won an Olympic Bronze Medal in 2016 and an Olympic Gold Medal in 2021.

At Rio 2016, she co-led Canada with three goals in five matches. She set a record for the fastest Olympic goal in the opener against Australia. Three days later, she scored two goals in a 3-1 win over Zimbabwe.

At the FIFA World Cup France 2019, Beckie started all four matches as Canada reached the Round of 16. She missed the 2023 FIFA World Cup through injury.

PORTLAND THORNS FC

Beckie joined Portland Thorns FC in 2022 and won her first NWSL Championship that year. She had previously played in England where she twice won the FA Cup and

twice won the FA League Cup with Manchester City FC. She was the first Canadian to score in the FA Cup Final at Wembley.

She missed most of the 2023 season through injury before she made it back onto the pitch with the start of the 2024 season.

CANADA RECORDS

"A" RECORDS	MP	MS	MIN	G	A
2014 CANADA	1	0	45		
2015 CANADA	8	4	384	3g	
2016 CANADA	16	13	1148	9g	3a
2017 CANADA	12	12	1003	8g	1a
2018 CANADA	11	10	837	4g	2a
2019 CANADA	15	12	1090	3g	2a
2020 CANADA	7	6	558	4g	2a
2021 CANADA	13	12	1028	2g	3a
2022 CANADA	15	14	1278	3g	4a
2022 CANADA	3	3	226		
FIRST 10 YEARS	101	86	7597	36g	4a

FIFA / OLYMPIC	MP	MS	MIN	G	A
2016 OLYMPIC	5	4	381	3g	1a
2019 FIFA WC	4	4	347		1a
2021 OLYMPIC	6	6	464	2g	
2023 FIFA WC	INJ				

2021 OLYMPIC GAMES • Janine Beckie scored both Canada goals in a 2-1 victory over Chile in the group phase at the Olympic Football Tournament in 2021. Two weeks later in the Final, she started up front on the wing when Canada captured their historic Gold Medal at Yokohama Stadium just south of Tokyo.

RIGHT BACK / F

JOSÉE BÉLANGER

Born: 1986-05-14, Coaticook, QC, CAN. Height 163 cm. Dominant right foot.

1 FIFA World Cup: Quarterfinals at Canada 2015
1 Olympic Games: Bronze at Rio 2016
2 Concacaf medals: Gold in 2010, Silver in 2016
1st #CANWNT: 2004-07-30 at Tokyo, JPN (v. JPN)
1st Goal: 2010-06-03 at Hamar, NOR (v. NOR)

OLYMPIC BRONZE MEDAL

Josée Bélanger represented Canada at one FIFA youth tournament, one FIFA World Cup and one Olympic Games. She helped Canada win a Concacaf youth title and a Concacaf Championship.

From late 2010 to early 2011, she helped Canada set a program record with an 11-match undefeated streak. Inside that streak, she helped Canada win the 2010 Concacaf Championship.

After she missed the 2011 FIFA World Cup through injury, she starred at Canada's home FIFA World Cup in 2015.

At Rio 2016, Bélanger won an Olympic Bronze Medal when Canada finished in third place. She missed the Semifinals against Germany through suspension, but was back in Canada's lineup for their last match.

CLUB CAREER

Bélanger played club football in Canada, Sweden and the United States. She won the 2015 Damallsvenskan in Sweden with FC Rosengård and was the first Canadian to score a UEFA Champions League hat trick when she beat PK-35 Vantaa three times in the Round of 32.

Bélanger played her college soccer at the Université de Sherbrooke where she was a three-time First Team All-Canadian.

CANADA RECORDS

"A" RECORDS	MP	MS	MIN	G	A
2004 CANADA	1	0	30		
2005 CANADA	0	0	0		
2009 CANADA	0	0	0		
2010 CANADA	10	10	744	5g	2a
2011 CANADA	0	0	0		
2013 CANADA	0	0	0		
2014 CANADA	11	8	667		
2015 CANADA	17	15	1310	2g	3a
2016 CANADA	17	10	1024		4a
2017 CANADA	1	1	57		
10 SEASONS	**57**	**44**	**3832**	**7g**	**9a**

FIFA / OLYMPIC	MP	MS	MIN	G	A
2011 FIFA WC	INJ	-	-		
2015 FIFA WC	5	5	450	1g	
2016 OLYMPIC	4	3	315		1a

● ● ●

2015 FIFA WORLD CUP • Josée Bélanger scored Canada's Round of 16 match winner at their home FIFA World Cup in front of a record-setting crowd of 53,855 spectators at BC Place. It was the largest crowd ever for a Canadian National Team event of any sport ever played in Canada (the attendance record was broken six days later in the Quarterfinals).

LEFT BACK

MELANIE BOOTH

Born: 1984-08-24, Burlington, ON, CAN. Height 175 cm. Dominant left foot.

1 FIFA World Cup: Group phase at China 2007
1 Olympic Games: Bronze at London 2012
4 Concacaf medals: Silver in 2002, 2006, 2008, 2012
1st #CANWNT: 2002-03-01 at Quarteira, POR (v. SCO)
1st Goal: 2006-11-22 FWCQ at Carson, CA, USA (v. JAM)

OLYMPIC BRONZE MEDAL

Melanie Booth represented Canada at the 2007 FIFA World Cup, won an Olympic Bronze Medal at London 2012, and won Bronze and Gold Medals at the Pan American Games in 2007 and 2011.

She won a FIFA Silver Medal at the first FIFA U-19 World Championship in 2002. In the Semifinals, she got the assist with her corner kick on Clare Rustad's 1-0 goal against Brazil.

In 2003, she helped Canada set a program record with a 10-match undefeated streak. In 2006, she scored her first goal at the Concacaf Gold Cup in the match that qualified Canada for the 2007 FIFA World Cup in China.

At back-to-back Pan American Games, she won a Bronze Medal at Rio 2007 and a Gold Medal at Guadalajara 2011. The following year, she was initially picked as a team alternate for the London 2012 Olympic Games, but she was added to the active roster through injuries.

CLUB CAREER

Booth played her club football in Canada and the United States. She reached the 2010 USL W-League Final with Vancouver Whitecaps FC and played in the inaugural NWSL season with Sky Blue FC. As a youth player, she won the 2002 U-17 Cup with the Burlington Flames.

CANADA RECORDS

"A" RECORDS	MP	MS	MIN	G	A
2002 CANADA	9	1	262		
2003 CANADA	6	4	360		1a
2006 CANADA	13	13	1200	1g	1a
2007 CANADA	5	4	319		1a
2008 CANADA	7	4	395		
2009 CANADA	5	5	405		
2010 CANADA	1	0	28		
2011 CANADA	11	3	396		
2012 CANADA	7	3	259		1a
2013 CANADA	2	0	31		
10 SEASONS	**66**	**37**	**3655**	**1g**	**4a**

FIFA / OLYMPIC	MP	MS	MIN	G	A
2007 FIFA WC	0	0	0		
2012 OLYMPIC	0	0	0		

2011 PAN AMERICAN GAMES • Melanie Booth made four appearances with Canada when they won a Gold Medal at the Pan American Games Guadalajara 2011 under new Head Coach John Herdman. She made three appearances as a substitute and got her one start in the 1-0 victory over Argentina.

MARY BETH BOWIE

Born: 1978-10-27, Halifax, NS, CAN. Grew up in Dartmouth, NS, CAN. Height 163 cm. Dominant right foot.

1 FIFA World Cup: Group phase at USA 1999
1st #CANWNT: 1999-05-21 at Burnaby, BC, CAN (v. MEX)

INTERNATIONAL CAREER

Mary Beth Bowie represented Canada at both the FIFA World Cup in 1999 and the Concacaf Gold Cup in 2000. At age 20, she was the youngest Canadian to feature at the 1999 FIFA World Cup.

In 1999, she made her international debut less than a month before the FIFA World Cup. She featured in the second half of a 3-0 win over Mexico at Swangard Stadium in Burnaby.

The following year, Bowie played six times for Canada including the fourth-place finish at the Concacaf Gold Cup. In the win over Guatemala, Bowie set up Christine Sinclair for her first of three goals for her first career international hat trick for Canada.

CLUB CAREER

Bowie played her club football in Canada where she lifted the Jubilee Trophy in 1999 and 2008 at Canada Soccer's National Championships. She won her first title with the Edmonton Angels and her second title with Halifax City.

Along with her two national titles, Bowie also reached the Canadian Final in 2004 with Halifax Athens United.

Bowie played her college soccer in her home province at Dalhousie University. In 1998, they finished third in the country at the CIAU Championship. She previously played her youth soccer in Halifax and Dartmouth.

Bowie was honoured by the Nova Scotia Sports Hall of Fame in 2018.

CANADA RECORDS

"A" RECORDS	MP	MS	MIN	G	A
1999 CANADA	7	2	266		
2000 CANADA	6	3	xx		1a
2001 CANADA	0	0	0		
2002 CANADA	0	0	0		
4 SEASONS	13	5	n/a		1a

FIFA / OLYMPIC	MP	MS	MIN	G	A
1999 FIFA WC	2	1	75		

● ● ●

1999 FIFA WORLD CUP • Mary Beth Bowie made two appearances at the 1999 FIFA Women's World Cup in the United States. She featured as a substitute in the second half of Canada's 7-1 loss to defending world champions Norway, then got the start up front in the 4-1 loss to Russia three days later.

③ BREANNA BOYD

RIGHT BACK / CB

Born: 1981-06-10, Edmonton, AB, CAN. Grew up in Calgary, AB, CAN. Height 172 cm. Dominant right foot.

Missed FIFA World Cup in 2003 through injury
1 Concacaf medal: Silver in 2002
1st #CANWNT: 2000-03-14 at Albufeira, POR (v. POR)
1st Goal: 2000-03-18 at Lagos, POR (v. DEN)

INTERNATIONAL CAREER

Breanna Boyd represented Canada at the 1999 Pan American Games as well as the 2000 and 2002 Concacaf Gold Cups. She was selected to represent Canada at the FIFA World Cup in 2003, but she missed the tournament recovering from a concussion.

In four years from 2000 to 2003, she made 43 international "A" appearances and scored goals against Denmark in 2000 and Portugal in 2001.

In November 2002, she played in all five Canada matches as they qualified for the FIFA World Cup before losing the Final to the United States on a golden goal.

CLUB CAREER

Boyd played her club football in Canada and the United States. She was drafted eighth overall in the 2003 WUSA Draft and turned pro with the Carolina Courage that FIFA World Cup season. She made 16 WUSA appearances and recorded two assists during her pro rookie season.

Boyd played her college soccer at the University of Nebraska in the United States. She was a three-time First-Team All-Big 12 Conference all-star from 2000 to 2002.

Boyd grew up playing her youth soccer in Calgary, notably the Calgary Foothills SC. She helped Alberta's U-18 team win a youth all-star championship in 1998.

CANADA RECORDS

"A" RECORDS	MP	MS	MIN	G	A
2000 CANADA	16	16	1452	1g	
2001 CANADA	12	12	1066	1g	
2002 CANADA	9	9	804		2a
2003 CANADA	6	6	514		1a
4 SEASONS	**43**	**43**	**3836**	**2g**	**3a**

FIFA / OLYMPIC	MP	MS	MIN	G	A
2003 FIFA WC	INJ	-	-		

2002 CONCACAF GOLD CUP • Breanna Boyd made four appearances when Canada finished in second place at the 2002 Concacaf Gold Cup. She featured in all three group matches in Victoria, missed the Semifinals in Seattle (after she took a ball to the face in training), and featured in the Final against the Americans at the Rose Bowl in Pasadena.

LEFT BACK / CB

SUE BRAND

Born: 1966-03-18, Edmonton, AB, CAN. Grew up in Nelson, BC, CAN & Edmonton. Height 163 cm. Dominant left foot.

1 FIFA International Tournament: Quarterfinals at China 1988
1 Concacaf medal: Silver in 1991
1st #CANWNT: 1987-12-11 at Kaohsiung City, TPE (v. HKG)

CANADA SOCCER HALL OF FAME

Sue Brand represented Canada at both the World Invitational Tournament in 1987 and FIFA's International Football Tournament in 1988. She won Silver at the first Concacaf Championship in 1991.

From 1987 to 1991, Brand made 20 career international "A" appearances for Canada. She was just 21 years old when she made her debut on 11 December 1987 in a 2-0 win over Hong Kong.

At the inaugural Concacaf Championship in 1991, Brand played every Canada minute when they finished in second place. Most matches were played in front of 30,000 to 40,000 spectators at Stade Sylvio Cator. At the time, only the champions USA qualified for the first FIFA Women's World Cup in 1991.

At the club level, Brand won five National Championships with the Edmonton Angels playing alongside her sister Anita Saiko. She missed Edmonton's first title in 1982, then lifted her first Jubilee Trophy in 1983

at age 17. She won more titles alongside her sister in 1984, 1985, 1986 and 1988. She won seven Alberta provincial titles from 1983 to 1990.

Growing up, Brand played her youth soccer in Edmonton, Alberta and Nelson, British Columbia. In 1966 when she was born, her father Joe played for the Western Canada League's first-place Edmonton Canadians SC.

CANADA RECORDS

"A" RECORDS	MP	MS	MIN	G	A
1987 CANADA	6	6	420		
1988 CANADA	4	4	320		
1989 CANADA	0	0	0		
1990 CANADA	5	5	400		
1991 CANADA	5	5	400		
5 SEASONS	**20**	**20**	**1540**		

FIFA / OLYMPIC	MP	MS	MIN	G	A
1988 FIFA	4	4	320		

● ● ●

1988 FIFA INTERNATIONAL TOURNAMENT • Sue Brand featured in every Canada minute at FIFA's first women's international football tournament in June 1988. Across three group matches, they lost 2-0 to the hosts China PR, won 6-0 over Côte d'Ivoire, and drew 1-1 with the Netherlands. They were eliminated in the Quarterfinals after a 1-0 loss to Sweden.

CENTRE BACK

KADEISHA BUCHANAN

Born: 1995-11-05, Toronto, ON, CAN. Grew up in Brampton, ON, CAN. Height 170 cm. Dominant right foot.

3 FIFA World Cups: Canada 2015, France 2019, AU NZ 2023
2 Olympic Games: Bronze at Rio 2016, Gold at Tokyo in 2021
4 Concacaf medals: Silver in 2016, 2018, 2020, 2022
1st #CANWNT: 2013-01-12 at Yongchuan, CHN (v. CHN)
1st Goal: 2014-05-08 at Winnipeg, MB, CAN (v. USA)

OLYMPIC CHAMPION

Kadeisha Buchanan has already played in two FIFA youth tournaments, three FIFA World Cups and two Olympic Games. She won Canada Soccer Player of the Year honours three times from 2015 to 2020.

She won an Olympic Bronze Medal in 2016 and an Olympic Gold Medal in 2021.

At her first FIFA World Cup in 2015, she played in every Canada minute and won the Best Young Player Award. At the FIFA World Cup in France, she played in every minute as Canada reached the Round of 16. She scored the 1-0 match winner in Canada's opening match against Cameroon.

At Rio 2016, she helped Canada post clean sheets against Australia in the first match and France in the Quarterfinals.

CHELSEA FC

Buchanan joined Chelsea FC in 2022-23 where she won the league title and FA Cup. In France, she played with FCF Olympique Lyonnais where she was a five-time UEFA Champions League winner. She won the league five times and the Cup three times.

Before moving to Europe, Buchanan played at West Virigina University.

CANADA RECORDS

"A" RECORDS	MP	MS	MIN	G	A
2012 CANADA	0	0	0		
2013 CANADA	15	12	1139		
2014 CANADA	11	11	990	1g	
2015 CANADA	18	17	1506	1g	1a
2016 CANADA	19	19	1682	1g	1a
2017 CANADA	9	9	791		
2018 CANADA	9	9	747		1a
2019 CANADA	14	13	1215	1g	
2020 CANADA	6	6	525		1a
2021 CANADA	12	12	1140		
2022 CANADA	15	15	1305		
2023 CANADA	12	12	1034		
FIRST 12 YEARS	**140**	**135**	**12,074**	**4g**	**4a**

FIFA / OLYMPIC	MP	MS	MIN	G	A
2015 FIFA WC	5	5	450		
2016 OLYMPIC	5	5	450		
2019 FIFA WC	4	4	360	1g	
2021 OLYMPIC	6	6	600		
2023 FIFA WC	3	3	225		

2021 OLYMPIC GAMES • Centre back Kadeisha Buchanan featured in every Canada minute across six matches at the 2021 Olympic Football Tournament in Japan. She helped Canada post clean sheets in the Quarterfinals against Brazil (before Canada won on kicks from the penalty mark) and the Semifinals against the United States (a 1-0 win).

FORWARD

17

SILVANA BURTINI

Born: 1969-05-10, Williams Lake, BC, CAN. Grew up in North Vancouver, BC, CAN. Height 170 cm. Dominant left foot.

1 FIFA International Tournament: Quarterfinals at China 1988
3 FIFA World Cups: Sweden 1995, USA 1999, USA 2003
4 Concacaf medals: Gold 1998, Silver 1994, 2002, Bronze 1993
1st #CANWNT: 1987-07-05 at Blaine, MN, USA (v. SWE)
1st Goal: 1993-08-04 at Long Island, NY, USA (v. TRI)

 CANADA SOCCER HALL OF FAME

Silvana Burtini represented Canada at three FIFA World Cups and she was part of their first Concacaf Championship in women's football. She also featured at FIFA's 1988 International Tournament in China three years before the first FIFA World Cup. When she left international football in 2003, she ranked third for Canada in both international appearances (77) and goals scored (38).

She was Canada Soccer's Player of the Year in 1998 and the runner up in both 1994 and 1995. She was the top scorer at the Concacaf Championship in both 1994 and 1998.

After she helped Canada reach FIFA's Quarterfinals in 1988, Burtini made her FIFA World Cup debut at Sweden 1995.

At the club level, Burtini played her football in Canada and the United States. In 1992 and 1993, she helped the Surrey Marlins win the Jubilee Trophy at Canada Soccer's National Championships.

Burtini later won her first USL W-League Championship with the Raleigh Wings in 1999. At the pro level, she played for the Carolina Courage in WUSA's inaugural 2001 season.

CANADA RECORDS

"A" RECORDS	MP	MS	MIN	G	A
1987 CANADA	2	1	xx		
1988 CANADA	3	2	173		1a
1993 CANADA	3	3	238	1g	
1994 CANADA	11	11	990	9g	
1995 CANADA	7	7	624	2g	1a
1997 CANADA	3	3	235	1g	
1998 CANADA	6	5	342	14g	2a
1999 CANADA	8	7	537	3g	1a
2000 CANADA	12	8	xx	4g	
2001 CANADA	5	3	xx	1g	
2002 CANADA	8	8	627	2g	2a
2003 CANADA	9	5	576	1g	1a
12 SEASONS	77	63	n/a	38g	8a

FIFA / OLYMPIC	MP	MS	MIN	G	A
1988 FIFA	3	2	173		
1995 FIFA WC	3	3	270	2g	1a
1999 FIFA WC	2	1	90	1g	
2003 FIFA WC	4	1	178		1a

● ● ●

FIFA WORLD CUPS • Silvana Burtini played in every minute of Canada's first FIFA World Cup in 1995, then featured in two matches in 1999 and four matches in 2003 when Canada finished in fourth place. She scored two goals in a 3-3 draw with Nigeria in 1995 and then scored one goal in a 1-1 draw with Japan in 1999.

MIDFIELDER

CONNIE CANT

Born: 1964-03-05, Montréal, QC, CAN. Grew up in St-Bruno, QC, CAN. Height 165 cm. Dominant left foot.

1 FIFA International Tournament: Quarterfinals at China 1988
1 Concacaf medal: Silver in 1991
1st #CANWNT: 1986-07-07 at Blaine, MN, USA (v. USA)
1st Goal: 1987-07-07 at Blaine, MN, USA (v. USA)

 ## CANADA SOCCER HALL OF FAME

Connie Cant represented Canada at both the World Invitational Tournament in 1987 and FIFA's International Football Tournament in 1988.

One of Canada's original National Team players from 1986 alongside sister Maureen Cant, Connie scored her first international goal against USA at the North America Cup in 1987.

In 1991, she featured in every minute as Canada took second place at the inaugural Concacaf Championship. At the time, only the champions USA qualified for the first FIFA World Cup in 1991.

Across six years from 1986 to 1991, Cant played in 22 of Canada's 24 international "A" matches. On 7 July 1986, she made her international debut in Canada's first-ever match against the Americans at the North America Cup.

At the club level, Cant played her football in Canada mostly with Dorval United SC. They won the 1989 National Championships Jubilee Trophy after they beat Oakville SC at King George V Park in St. John's.

At college, Cant played for Concordia University in Montréal. She was a CIAU First Team All-Canadian in 1988.

CANADA RECORDS

"A" RECORDS	MP	MS	MIN	G	A
1986 CANADA	2	2	180		
1987 CANADA	7	7	xx	1g	
1988 CANADA	4	4	295	1g	
1989 CANADA	0	0	0		
1990 CANADA	5	5	400	1g	
1991 CANADA	4	4	320	1g	
6 SEASONS	**22**	**22**	**n/a**	**4g**	

FIFA / OLYMPIC	MP	MS	MIN	G	A
1988 FIFA	4	4	295	1g	

1988 FIFA INTERNATIONAL TOURNAMENT • Connie Cant featured in all four Canada matches at FIFA's first women's international tournament in June 1988. She scored one goal in the tournament, Canada's last in a 6-0 victory over Côte d'Ivoire. Canada went on to reach the Quarterfinals, but were eliminated after a narrow 1-0 loss to Sweden.

FULLBACK / M

21

GABRIELLE CARLE

Born: 1998-10-12, Québec, QC, CAN. Grew up in Lévis, QC, CAN. Height 168 cm. Dominant right foot.

2 FIFA World Cups: France 2019, AU NZ 2023
1 Olympic Games: Gold at Tokyo in 2021
3 Concacaf medals: Silver in 2016, 2018, 2020
1st #CANWNT: 2015-12-09 at Natal, BRA (v. MEX)
1st Goal: 2016-02-16 FWCQ at Houston, TX, USA (v. GUA)

OLYMPIC CHAMPION

Gabrielle Carle has already represented Canada at two FIFA youth tournaments, two FIFA World Cups and one Olympic Games. She was also one of Canada's alternates at the Rio 2016 Olympic Games. She twice finished as a runner up in voting for Canada Soccer's U-20 Player of the Year award.

She scored her first international goal at the 2016 Concacaf Olympic Qualifiers against Guatemala.

In 2021, she helped Canada set a program record with a 12-match undefeated streak that included their historic Olympic Gold Medal.

WASHINGTON SPIRIT

Carle joined the Washington Spirit in the National Women's Soccer League ahead of the 2023 season. One year earlier, she had spent her pro rookie season in Sweden with fourth-place Kristianstads DFF. In UEFA Champions League Qualifying, she scored two goals in two matches.

Before turning pro, Carle played her college soccer at Florida State University. She won the NCAA Championship in 2018 and 2021.

CANADA RECORDS

"A" RECORDS	MP	MS	MIN	G	A
2015 CANADA	2	1	91		
2016 CANADA	5	2	217	1g	1a
2017 CANADA	2	1	70		
2018 CANADA	1	0	31		
2019 CANADA	5	2	206		
2020 CANADA	5	3	259		
2021 CANADA	8	5	433		
2022 CANADA	7	1	241		
2023 CANADA	3	0	60		1a
FIRST 9 YEARS	**38**	**15**	**1608**	**1g**	**2a**

FIFA / OLYMPIC	MP	MS	MIN	G	A
2016 OLYMPIC	-	-	-		
2019 FIFA WC	0	0	0		
2021 OLYMPIC	1	0	10		
2023 FIFA WC	0	0	0		

● ● ●

2021 OLYMPIC GAMES • Gabrielle Carle made one appearance at the Olympic Football Tournament in 2021 when Canada won their historic Gold Medal in Japan. She featured as a substitute in Canada's group finale when they drew 1-1 with Great Britain. With the point, Canada finished second in their group and officially qualified for the knockout phase.

ANNIE CARON

Born: 1964-05-06, St-Foy, QC, CAN. Grew up in Dollard-des-Ormeaux, QC, CAN. Height 160 cm. Dominant right foot.

1 FIFA International Tournament: Quarterfinals at China 1988
1 FIFA World Cup: Group phase at Sweden 1995
2 Concacaf medals: Silver in 1991 and 1994
1st #CANWNT: 1986-07-07 at Blaine, MN, USA (v. USA)
1st Goal: 1987-07-07 at Blaine, MN, USA (v. USA)

CANADA SOCCER HALL OF FAME

Annie Caron represented Canada at their first FIFA World Cup in 1995 after featuring at both the World Invitational Tournament in 1987 and FIFA's International Football Tournament in 1988.

Across her career from 1986 to 1995, she made 34 international "A" appearances, which at the time ranked tied for fourth all time for Canada. She was just 22 years old when she made her international debut in Canada's first-ever match at the 1986 North America Cup.

She scored her first international goal in a 4-2 loss to the Americans at the 1987 North America Cup. One year later, she scored two goals in a 6-0 win over Côte d'Ivoire at the 1988 International Football Tournament.

At the first two Concacaf Championships in 1991 and 1994, she helped Canada finish in second place. While only the champions qualified for the FIFA World Cup in 1991, both USA and Canada qualified in 1994 for the FIFA World Cup in 1995.

At the club level, Caron played her football in Canada and Italy. She won the Jubilee Trophy at the 1989 National Championships with Dorval United SC.

She played her college soccer in Montréal at Concordia University where she was a three-time CIAU First Team All-Canadian.

CANADA RECORDS

"A" RECORDS	MP	MS	MIN	G	A
1986 CANADA	2	0	96		
1987 CANADA	5	5	365	1g	
1988 CANADA	4	4	320	2g	1a
1989 CANADA	0	0	0		
1990 CANADA	0	0	0		
1991 CANADA	5	4	308	4g	
1994 CANADA	10	9	561		
1995 CANADA	8	5	462	1g	
8 SEASONS	**34**	**27**	**2112**	**8g**	**1a**

FIFA / OLYMPIC	MP	MS	MIN	G	A
1988 FIFA	4	4	320	2g	
1995 FIFA WC	2	2	167		

1995 FIFA WORLD CUP • Annie Caron made two appearances at the FIFA Women's World Cup in Sweden, making her one of six original Women's National Team players who also represented Canada at their first FIFA World Cup in 1995. She featured in Canada's 3-3 draw with Nigeria as well as their 7-0 loss to 1995 world champions Norway.

LEFT BACK

2

ALLYSHA CHAPMAN

Born: 1989-01-25, Oshawa, ON, CAN. Grew up in Courtice, ON, CAN. Height 161 cm. Dominant left foot.

3 FIFA World Cups: Canada 2015, France 2019, AU NZ 2023
2 Olympic Games: Bronze at Rio 2016, Gold at Tokyo in 2021
4 Concacaf medals: Silver in 2016, 2018, 2020, 2022
1st #CANWNT: 2014-10-25 at Edmonton, AB, CAN (v. JPN)
1st Goal: 2015-03-09 at Nicosia, CYP (v. ITA)

OLYMPIC CHAMPION

Allysha Chapman has already played in one FIFA youth tournament, three FIFA World Cups and two Olympic Games. In 2008, she helped Canada win the Concacaf Under-20 Championship.

She won an Olympic Bronze Medal in 2016 and an Olympic Gold Medal in 2021.

At three FIFA World Cups from 2015 to 2023, she played in every Canada match. They reached the Quarterfinals at Canada 2015 and the Round of 16 at France 2019.

In 2022, Chapman scored her second career international goal in the Semifinals at the Concacaf W Championship.

HOUSTON DASH

Chapman turned pro in 2012 in Sweden, but then joined the Houston Dash for the first time in 2015. After stints with Boston and North Carolina, she rejoined Houston in 2018 and she won the NWSL Challenge Cup in 2020. They also finished second in the 2020 NWSL Fall Series standings.

Before moving overseas, Chapman played her college soccer at Louisiana State University where she won Louisiana Player of the Year honours in 2010. She spent most of her W-League career with the Toronto Lady Lynx.

CANADA RECORDS

"A" RECORDS		MP	MS	MIN	G	A
2009	CANADA	0	0	0		
2014	CANADA	3	2	210		
2015	CANADA	18	16	1472	1g	1a
2016	CANADA	18	9	913		1a
2017	CANADA	8	8	633		
2018	CANADA	10	9	785		1a
2019	CANADA	12	10	725		
2020	CANADA	6	4	358		
2021	CANADA	11	11	967		
2022	CANADA	7	2	284	1g	
2023	CANADA	6	3	253		
FIRST 11 YEARS		**99**	**74**	**6600**	**2g**	**3a**

FIFA / OLYMPIC		MP	MS	MIN	G	A
2015	FIFA WC	5	5	450		
2016	OLYMPIC	5	2	238		
2019	FIFA WC	4	3	258		
2021	OLYMPIC	4	4	382		
2023	FIFA WC	3	0	65		

● ● ●

2021 OLYMPIC GAMES • Allysha Chapman made four appearances at the Olympic Football Tournament when Canada won their historic Gold Medal in Japan. In the knockout phase, she helped Canada post back-to-back clean sheets against Brazil and USA. In the Final, Canada drew 1-1 with Sweden before they won 3-2 in the shootout to capture Gold.

9

CANDACE CHAPMAN

CENTRE BACK

Born: 1983-04-02, Port of Spain, TRI. Grew up in Ajax, ON, CAN. Height 170 cm. Dominant right foot.

2 FIFA World Cups: China 2007, Germany 2011
2 Olympic Games: Beijing 2008, Bronze at London 2012
5 Concacaf medals: Gold 2010, Silver 2002, 2006, 2008, 2012
1st #CANWNT: 2002-03-01 at Quarteira, POR (v. SCO)
1st Goal: 2002-10-30 FWCQ at Victoria, BC, CAN (v. HAI)

CANADA SOCCER HALL OF FAME

Candace Chapman won a Bronze Medal from two Olympic Games, featured in two FIFA World Cups, and won a Concacaf Championship as an international player. She retired ranked seventh all time with 114 career international appearances for Canada.

She won a Silver Medal from the first FIFA U-19 World Championship in 2002 and was named a tournament all-star.

She twice helped Canada set program records for unbeaten streaks (2003 and 2010-11). She missed the 2003 FIFA World Cup through injury, but scored goals at the 2007 FIFA World Cup and 2008 Olympic Games.

At the club level, she played her football in Canada and the United States. She won back-to-back WPS Championships in 2010 and 2011, the first with FC Gold Pride and the second with the Western New York Flash. She also helped both teams win regular-season titles.

In 2006 with the Vancouver Whitecaps, she missed the USL W-League Championship through injury.

In her last professional season in 2013, she played for the Washington Spirit during the NWSL's inaugural campaign.

CANADA RECORDS

"A" RECORDS	MP	MS	MIN	G	A
2002 CANADA	10	10	891	1g	1a
2003 CANADA	11	8	737		1a
2005 CANADA	4	3	333		
2006 CANADA	6	4	365		
2007 CANADA	8	7	630	3g	1a
2008 CANADA	23	22	2026	1g	2a
2009 CANADA	3	3	265		
2010 CANADA	13	13	1131	1g	1a
2011 CANADA	19	18	1700		1a
2012 CANADA	17	15	1357		1a
10 SEASONS	**114**	**103**	**9435**	**6g**	**8a**

FIFA / OLYMPIC	MP	MS	MIN	G	A
2003 FIFA WC	INJ	-	-		
2007 FIFA WC	3	3	253	1g	1a
2008 OLYMPIC	4	4	390	1g	
2011 FIFA WC	3	3	270		
2012 OLYMPIC	2	1	97		

2012 OLYMPIC GAMES • Candace Chapman was injured in the opening match of the London 2012 Olympic Football Tournament, but she worked her way back into the lineup two weeks later before the last day of the tournament. On that last day, she featured at centre back in the last seven-plus minutes of Canada's 1-0 victory over France.

GOALKEEPER

CARLA CHIN BAKER

Born: 1996-05-10, Kingston, JAM. Grew up in Scarborough & Aurora, ON, CAN. Height 165 cm. Dominant right foot.

1 FIFA International Tournament: Quarterfinals at China 1988
1 FIFA World Cup: Group phase at Sweden 1995
2 Concacaf medals: Silver in 1991 and 1994
1st #CANWNT: 1987-12-11 at Kaohsiung City, TPE (v. HKG)
1st Clean Sheet: 1987-12-11 at Kaohsiung City, TPE (v. HKG)

CANADA SOCCER HALL OF FAME

Carla Chin represented Canada at their first FIFA World Cup in 1995 after featuring at both the World Invitational Tournament in 1987 and FIFA's International Football Tournament in 1988.

One of Canada's original Women's National Team players from 1986, she posted her first clean sheet in her first official "A" match against Hong Kong in 1987.

After 12 years as one of Canada's best goalkeepers, she left international football as Canada's all-time leader in appearances by a goalkeeper (29) and clean sheets (eight).

Chin helped Canada finish in second place at the Concacaf Championship in both 1991 and 1994. She featured in every minute of the 1991 tournament and posted four clean sheets in five matches.

Chin played her club football in Canada and the United States. She helped Oakville SC finish as runners up at the National Championships in both 1987 and 1989. With the Ontario Selects, she won Canada Soccer's 1986 and 1987 Women's All-Star Championship in Winnipeg.

Chin played her college soccer at McMaster University where she helped her school reach the 1987 CIAU Final.

CANADA RECORDS

"A" RECORDS		MP	MS	MIN	G	A
1986	CANADA	0	0	0		
1987	CANADA	4	4	280	1	CS
1988	CANADA	2	2	160	1	CS
1989	CANADA	0	0	0		
1990	CANADA	4	4	320	1	CS
1991	CANADA	5	5	400	4	CS
1993	CANADA	3	3	212	0	CS
1994	CANADA	1	1	90	0	CS
1995	CANADA	10	10	906	1	CS
1997	CANADA	0	0	0		
10 SEASONS		**29**	**29**	**2368**	**8**	**CS**

FIFA / OLYMPIC		MP	MS	MIN		CS
1988	FIFA	2	2	160		1 CS
1995	FIFA WC	3	3	270		0 CS

● ● ●

1995 FIFA WORLD CUP • Carla Chin Baker was in goal for all three Canada group matches at the FIFA Women's World Cup Sweden 1995. It was Canada Soccer's Women's National Team's first participation at the FIFA World Cup. Canada lost 3 2 to England (with two goals scored on penalties), drew 3-3 with Nigeria, and lost 7-0 to the champions Norway.

GOALKEEPER

18

SABRINA D'ANGELO

Born: 1993-05-11, Welland, ON, CAN.   Height 173 cm. Dominant left foot.

2 FIFA World Cups: France 2019, AU NZ 2023
1 Olympic Games: Bronze at Rio 2016
3 Concacaf medals: Silver in 2016, 2020, 2022
1st #CANWNT: 2016-03-04 at Real Santo Antonio, POR (v. BEL)
1st Clean Sheet: 2016-03-04 at Real Santo Antonio, POR (v. BEL)

OLYMPIC BRONZE MEDAL

Sabrina D'Angelo has already played for Canada at three FIFA youth tournaments, two FIFA World Cups and one Olympic Games. She won the Concacaf Under-17 Championship in 2010 and was Canada Soccer's U-20 Player of the Year in 2012.

She won an Olympic Bronze Medal in 2016.

Before the Rio 2016 Olympic Games, she posted her first clean sheet in her Canada debut against Belgium, a 1-0 win at the Algarve Cup. Five days later, she was in goal when Canada won 2-1 over Brazil to clinch their first Algarve Cup title.

ARSENAL FC

D'Angelo joined Arsenal FC in 2022-23 and helped the team finish third overall in the FA Women's Super League. She helped Arsenal FC with the League Cup in both 2023 and 2024.

Before moving to England, D'Angelo played her club football in Canada, USA and Sweden. She won the NWSL Champion-ship with the North Carolina Courage in 2016 and 2018. She also won the NWSL Shield in 2017 and 2018.

In Sweden, she helped Vittsjö GIK finish third in the standings in 2019.

CANADA RECORDS

"A" RECORDS	MP	MS	MIN		CS
2010 CANADA	0	0	0		
2012 CANADA	0	0	0		
2015 CANADA	0	0	0		
2016 CANADA	3	2	225	1	CS
2017 CANADA	2	1	135	1	CS
2018 CANADA	0	0	0		
2019 CANADA	2	1	135	1	CS
2020 CANADA	1	1	90	1	CS
2021 CANADA	0	0	0		
2022 CANADA	4	2	270	2	CS
2023 CANADA	2	2	120	1	CS
FIRST 11 YEARS	14	9	975	7	CS

FIFA / OLYMPIC	MP	MS	MIN		CS
2016 OLYMPIC	1	1	90	0	CS
2019 FIFA WC	0	0	0		
2023 FIFA WC	0	0	0		

2016 OLYMPIC GAMES • Goalkeeper Sabrina D'Angelo made one appearance when Canada won their second Bronze Medal at the Olympic Football Tournament in 2016. After Stephanie Labbé was in goal for the first win against Australia, D'Angelo was in goal for the second win against Zimbabwe to secure Canada's spot in the Quarterfinals.

RIGHT BACK / CB

TRACY DAVID

Born: 1960-01-21, Pouce Coupe, BC, CAN. Grew up in Toms-lake, BC, CAN. Height 159 cm. Dominant right foot.

1st #CANWNT: 1986-07-07 Blaine, MN, USA (v. USA)

CANADA SOCCER HALL OF FAME

Tracy David was an original member of Canada's National Team in 1986 and she represented her country a year later at the 1987 World Invitational Tournament.

In the program's first four years, she made seven international "A" appearances, but played 12 in total including tournament matches against clubs or against the US youth team.

She represented Canada at the North America Cup in July 1986 and July 1987, the World Invitational in December 1987, and a tour against Danish clubs in July 1989.

She was Canada's starting right back for their first two international matches against USA at the 1986 North America Cup in Blaine. Canada lost the first match 2-0, but won the second match 2-1 on two goals by Geri Donnelly.

David played her club football in Canada where she won a joint-record six National Championships from 1982 to 1988 with the Edmonton Angels. David and Anita Saiko won six titles in that span. Goalkeeper Sue Simon joined David and Saiko in that exclusive group when she won her sixth title in 1995.

David and the Angels won five-straight titles from 1982 to 1986, finished third in 1987, then won their sixth title in 1988. David then had two more third-place finishes with Edmonton International Azzurre in 1991 and 1992.

As a youth player, she helped Edmonton Ajax reach Canada Soccer's U-18 Final in 1978.

CANADA RECORDS

"A" RECORDS	MP	MS	MIN	G	A
1986 CANADA	2	2	180		
1987 CANADA	5	5	390		
1989 CANADA	0	0	0		
3 SEASONS	7	7	570		

● ● ●

1986 NORTH AMERICA CUP • Tracy David made her Canada debut in their first international series back in 1986 against the United States at the North American Cup. Canada lost the first match 2-0, came back to win the second match 2-1, but then lost the series after the Americans won a 30-minute mini match immediately following Canada's 2-1 win.

TANYA DENNIS

RIGHT BACK

Born: 1985-08-26, Brampton, ON, CAN. Height 168 cm.

2 FIFA World Cups: China 2007, 4th Place at USA 2003
1 Concacaf medal: Bronze in 2004
1st #CANWNT: 2003-08-31 at Edmonton, AB, CAN (v MEX)

INTERNATIONAL CAREER

Tanya Dennis represented Canada at one FIFA youth tournament and two FIFA World Cups, notably helping Canada finish in fourth place at the 2003 FIFA World Cup in the United States.

Shortly before the FIFA World Cup, she helped Canada's U-23 squad win a Silver Medal at the Pan American Games in Santo Domingo. From that team, she was one of five Canadians that made the jump from the U-23 squad in August to the FIFA World Cup squad in September.

When she made her international "A" debut on 31 August against Mexico, Canada were just three weeks away from the start of the FIFA World Cup.

Across five years from 2003 to 2007, she made 18 career international appearances.

CLUB CAREER

Dennis played soccer in Canada and the United States where she was enrolled at the University of Nebraska. She was a First

Team All-Big 12 selection in 2004 and a Second Team All-Big selection in 2006.

As a teenager in 2002, she helped Oakville SC lift the Jubilee Trophy at Canada Soccer's National Championships.

Dennis helped Ontario's U-17 team win two youth all-star championships in 2000 and 2002. She also won a Gold Medal at the 2001 Canada Games.

CANADA RECORDS

"A" RECORDS	MP	MS	MIN	G	A
2003 CANADA	8	8	713		
2004 CANADA	4	1	120		
2005 CANADA	1	0	17		
2006 CANADA	0	0	0		
2007 CANADA	5	5	426		
5 SEASONS	**18**	**14**	**1276**		

FIFA / OLYMPIC	MP	MS	MIN	G	A
2003 FIFA WC	5	5	450		
2007 FIFA WC	3	3	270		

FIFA WORLD CUPS • Tanya Dennis featured in eight of Canada's nine matches across back-to-back FIFA World Cups at USA 2003 and China 2007. She helped Canada finish in fourth place in 2003, which included a memorable 1-0 win over China PR in the Quarterfinals. Dennis only missed the last match of that tournament against USA because of a concussion.

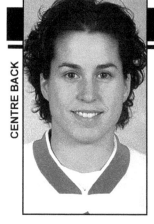

CENTRE BACK

8

MARIE-CLAUDE DION

Born: 1974-04-25, Québec, QC, CAN. Height 165 cm. Dominant right foot.

Missed FIFA World Cup in 1999 through injury
1 Concacaf medal: Gold in 1998
1st #CANWNT: 1996-05-12 at Worcester, MA, USA (v. USA)

CONCACAF CHAMPION

Marie-Claude Dion helped Canada win the 1998 Concacaf Championship in Toronto when they also qualified for the 1999 FIFA World Cup. She missed that FIFA World Cup through injury, but was back a year later with Canada for a fourth-place finish at the 2000 Concacaf Gold Cup.

With Canada from 1993 to 2001, Dion made 27 career international "A" appearances. She was just 22 years old when she made her Canada "A" debut on 12 May 1996 against the United States.

In 1993, she represented Canada at the World University Games in Hamilton. In 2001, she made her last international appearance in a 2-1 win over Portugal at the Algarve Cup.

CLUB CAREER

Dion played her club football in Canada and the United States. She won back-to-back league titles with Dynamo de Québec in 1995 and 1996. They won the Coupe du Québec provincial title in 1996.

At the Université de Laval, Dion reached the CIAU Championship in 1996 and 1997, but did not win a national medal in either year. She won the Chantal Navert Memorial Award in 1996 as the nation's top university player.

She played her youth soccer in her home province of Québec.

CANADA RECORDS

"A" RECORDS		MP	MS	MIN	G	A
1993	CANADA	0	0	0		
1996	CANADA	5	5	450		
1997	CANADA	3	3	173		
1998	CANADA	8	8	609		
1999	CANADA	2	2	180		
2000	CANADA	8	7	654		
2001	CANADA	1	1	56		
7 SEASONS		27	26	2122		

FIFA / OLYMPIC	MP	MS	MIN	G	A
1999 FIFA WC	INJ	-	-		

● ● ●

1998 CONCACAF CHAMPIONSHIP • Marie-Claude Dion featured in all five matches when Canada won the 1998 Concacaf Championship at Centennial Stadium in Toronto. She made five starts and helped Canada post five-straight clean sheets. The following year, she missed the 1999 FIFA World Cup after she suffered a knee injury just before the tournament.

MIDFIELDER

6

GERI DONNELLY

Born: 1965-11-30, London, ENG. Grew up in Port Moody, BC, CAN. Height 163 cm. Shot left and right foot.

1 FIFA International Tournament: Quarterfinals at China 1988
2 FIFA World Cups: Group phase at Sweden 1995 and USA 1999
4 Concacaf medals: Gold 1998, Silver 1991, 1994, Bronze 1993
1st #CANWNT: 1986-07-07 at Blaine, MN, USA (v. USA)
1st Goal: 1986-07-09 at Blaine, MN, USA (v. USA)

CANADA SOCCER HALL OF FAME

Geri Donnelly represented Canada at two FIFA World Cups as well as FIFA's first International Football Tournament in 1988. She won four Concacaf medals and lifted the Concacaf Championship trophy in 1998. She was Canada Soccer's Player of the Year in 1999.

One of Canada's original Women's National Team players from 1986, Donnelly scored the program's first two goals in their first win over USA on 9 July 1986. She also scored in Canada's first FIFA World Cup match on 6 June 1995.

Across her Canada career from 1986 to 2000, she set a national record when she made 71 international "A" appearances. She also set a record with 33 consecutive Canada appearances from 1993 to 1997.

After she left international football, she was awarded Canada Soccer's Aubrey Sanford Meritorious Service Award in 2002. She continued to play club football until the end of 2009.

She won the Jubilee Trophy three times at Canada Soccer's National Championships. She won her first Canadian title in 1990 with the Coquitlam Strikers, her second title in 1994 with Coquitlam Metro-Ford SC, and her third title in 2006 with Surrey United SC.

CANADA RECORDS

"A" RECORDS	MP	MS	MIN	G	A
1986 CANADA	1	1	90	2g	
1987 CANADA	8	8	xx		
1988 CANADA	4	4	320		
1989 CANADA	0	0	0		
1990 CANADA	5	5	400	3g	
1991 CANADA	5	5	353		
1993 CANADA	3	3	270		
1994 CANADA	11	11	990	1g	
1995 CANADA	12	12	1031	2g	
1996 CANADA	5	5	450		
1997 CANADA	2	2	169		
1998 CANADA	4	0	169		
1999 CANADA	11	9	832	1g	1a
2000 CANADA	0	0	0		
14 SEASONS	**71**	**65**	**n/a**	**9g**	**1a**

FIFA / OLYMPIC	MP	MS	MIN	G	A
1988 FIFA	4	4	320		
1995 FIFA WC	3	3	270	2g	
1999 FIFA WC	3	3	270		1a

FIFA WORLD CUPS • Geri Donnelly played every minute of Canada's six group matches across back-to-back FIFA World Cups at Sweden 1995 and USA 1999. She scored Canada's second goal in the 3-2 loss to England on 6 June 1995, then scored again in a 3-3 draw with Nigeria just two days later.

FORWARD

JONELLE FILIGNO

Born: 1990-09-24, Mississauga, ON, CAN. Height 168 cm. Dominant right foot.

2 FIFA World Cups: Germany 2011, Canada 2015
2 Olympic Games: Beijing 2008, Bronze at London 2012
2 Concacaf medals: Gold in 2010, Silver in 2008
1st #CANWNT: 2008-01-16 at Guangzhou, CHN (v. USA)
1st Goal: 2008-04-02 OQ at Juárez, CH, MEX (v. TRI)

OLYMPIC BRONZE MEDAL

Jonelle Filigno represented Canada at one FIFA youth tournament, two FIFA World Cups and two Olympic Games. She won an Olympic Bronze Medal at London 2012.

In 2008, she played 32 matches back and forth between the Women's National Team and the U-20 squad. She made her "A" debut in January, won a Concacaf youth title in June, made her Olympic debut in August, and featured at the FIFA U-20 World Cup in November. She won Canada Soccer's U-20 Player of the Year award in both 2008 and 2010.

From late 2010 to early 2011, she helped Canada set a program record with an 11-match undefeated streak. Inside that streak, she helped Canada win the 2010 Concacaf Championship.

From 2008 to 2015, she scored 11 goals in 71 career international "A" appearances. She was just 17 years old when she scored her first "A" goal against Trinidad & Tobago in 2008. She made her FIFA World Cup debut in 2011 and she reached the FIFA World Cup Quarterfinals in 2015.

CLUB CAREER

Filigno played her club football in Canada and the United States. She turned pro in 2014 and spent two seasons with the NWSL's Sky Blue FC.

She was honoured by the Rutgers Athletics Hall of Fame in 2020.

CANADA RECORDS

"A" RECORDS	MP	MS	MIN	G	A
2008 CANADA	20	12	1094	1g	
2009 CANADA	2	2	148		
2010 CANADA	5	1	220	4g	2a
2011 CANADA	15	15	1155	3g	2a
2012 CANADA	8	4	337	1g	
2013 CANADA	5	5	356	1g	1a
2014 CANADA	7	2	244	1g	
2015 CANADA	9	4	342		
8 SEASONS	71	45	3896	11g	5a

FIFA / OLYMPIC	MP	MS	MIN	G	A
2008 OLYMPIC	3	0	39		
2011 FIFA WC	3	3	236		
2012 OLYMPIC	5	4	271	1g	
2015 FIFA WC	3	2	145		

● ● ●

2012 OLYMPIC GAMES • Jonelle Filigno made five appearances when Canada won their inspiring Bronze Medal at the Olympic Football Tournament in 2012. In the Quarterfinals at the City of Coventry Stadium, Filigno scored the match winner in the 12th minute when she redirected a Sophie Schmidt corner kick past Great Britain's Karen Bardsley.

17

JESSIE FLEMING

MIDFIELDER

Born: 1998-03-11, London, ON, CAN.   Height 164 cm. Dominant right foot.

3 FIFA World Cups: Canada 2015, France 2019, AU NZ 2023
2 Olympic Games: Bronze at Rio 2016, Gold at Tokyo in 2021
4 Concacaf medals: Silver in 2016, 2018, 2020, 2022
1st #CANWNT: 2013-12-15 at Brasilia, BRA (v. CHI)
1st Goal: 2015-03-04 at Nicosia, CYP (v. SCO)

OLYMPIC CHAMPION

Jessie Fleming has already represented Canada at two FIFA youth tournaments, three FIFA World Cups and two Olympic Games. She won Canada Soccer's Player of the Year award three-straight seasons from 2021 to 2023.

She won an Olympic Bronze Medal in 2016 and an Olympic Gold Medal in 2021. She was Canada's Player of the Match in the Gold Medal Final at Tokyo in 2021.

In 2015, she made her FIFA World Cup debut in the opening match against China PR at Edmonton. Across three FIFA World Cups from 2015 to 2023, she has made eight appearances. She scored her first FIFA World Cup goal at France 2019.

Fleming was named to the Best XI at the Concacaf Championship in 2022 as well as the Concacaf Gold Cup in 2024.

PORTLAND THORNS FC

Fleming joined Portland Thorns FC ahead of the 2024 season.

In England with Chelsea FC, she was a three-time FA Cup winner (2021, 2022, 2023), a three-time FA Women's Super League winner (2020-21, 2021-22, 2022-23), and a one-time FA League Cup winner (2020-21)

CANADA RECORDS

"A" RECORDS		MP	MS	MIN	G	A
2013	CANADA	2	1	63		
2014	CANADA	6	3	292		
2015	CANADA	13	9	684	1g	
2016	CANADA	15	11	984	2g	1a
2017	CANADA	11	11	990	1g	1a
2018	CANADA	10	10	894	3g	2a
2019	CANADA	13	13	1162	2g	
2020	CANADA	7	6	514	1g	
2021	CANADA	17	16	1481	4g	1a
2022	CANADA	17	17	1420	5g	
2023	CANADA	12	11	905		1a
FIRST 11 YEARS		**123**	**108**	**9389**	**19g**	**6a**

FIFA / OLYMPIC		MP	MS	MIN	G	A
2015	FIFA WC	2	1	80		
2016	OLYMPIC	6	6	475		1a
2019	FIFA WC	4	4	360	1g	
2021	OLYMPIC	6	5	555	2g	
2023	FIFA WC	2	2	180		

2021 OLYMPIC GAMES • Jessie Fleming featured in all six Canada matches when they won their historic Gold Medal at Yokohama Stadium in Japan. She scored penalty goals in the last two matches of the tournament: the 1-0 winner against USA in the Semifinals; and the 1-1 equaliser in the Final against Sweden (before Canada won 3-2 in the shootout).

FULLBACK / M

4

TANYA FRANCK

Born: 1974-12-13, North York, ON, CAN. Grew up in Scarborough, ON, CAN. Height 168 cm. Dominant right foot.

1 FIFA World Cup: Group phase at USA 1999
1 Concacaf medal: Gold in 1998
1st #CANWNT: 1997-05-31 at New Britain, CT, USA (v. USA)
1st Goal: 1998-08-28 FWCQ at Toronto, ON, CAN (v. PUR)

CONCACAF CHAMPION

Tanya Franck represented Canada at the FIFA World Cup in 1999 after she won the Concacaf Championship in 1998. She also represented Canada at the Concacaf Gold Cup in 2000.

She was 22 years old when she made her international debut on 31 May 1997 in a 4-0 loss to the United States. She scored her first two Canada goals in a lopsided win over Puerto Rico at the 1998 Concacaf Championship in Toronto.

In all, Franck played 29 international "A" matches for Canada from 1997 to 2000. She made her last appearance at the 2000 Concacaf Gold Cup and she scored a goal in the 12-0 win over Guatemala.

CLUB CAREER

Franck played her club football in Canada, USA and Germany. In 1995, she helped her hometown club Scarborough Azzurri finish in third place at Canada Soccer's National Championships. In 1998-99, she played in Germany's Bundesliga at FFC Heike

Rheine alongside Canadian teammate Liz Smith.

Franck played her college soccer in the United States at the University of Nebraska. She served as the team's co-captain.

At the youth level, she helped Scarborough United win Canada Soccer's U-14 Cup in 1988 and the U-18 Cup in 1992. They also finished in third place at the U-16 Cup in 1990.

CANADA RECORDS

"A" RECORDS	MP	MS	MIN	G	A
1997 CANADA	3	3	280		
1998 CANADA	7	7	528	2g	
1999 CANADA	11	11	920		1a
2000 CANADA	8	7	532	1g	
4 SEASONS	29	28	2260	3g	1a

FIFA / OLYMPIC	MP	MS	MIN	G	A
1999 FIFA WC	3	3	270		

● ● ●

1999 FIFA WORLD CUP • Tanya Franck featured in every Canada minute at the 1999 FIFA Women's World Cup in the United States. After a 1-1 draw with Japan in their opening match, they lost 7-1 to Norway and 4-1 to Russia. Just one year earlier, Franck helped Canada post five-straight clean sheets to win the 1998 Concacaf Championship in Toronto.

10

CENTRE BACK / F

MARTINA FRANKO

Née Martina Holan. Born: 1976-01-13, Cincinnati, OH, USA. Grew up in Los Altos, CA, USA. Ht. 172 cm. Dominant right foot.

1 FIFA World Cup: Group phase at China 2007
1 Olympic Games: Quarterfinals at Beijing 2008
2 Concacaf medals: Silver in 2006 and 2008
1st #CANWNT: 2005-09-01 at Burnaby, BC, CAN (v. GER)
1st Goal: 2005-09-04 at Edmonton, AB, CAN (v. GER)

CANADA SOCCER HALL OF FAME

Martina Franko represented Canada at the 2007 FIFA World Cup and 2008 Olympic Games. Initially a forward who excelled with Canada at centre back, she made 55 career appearances at the international level in a five-year span.

From her debut in 2005, she featured in 41 consecutive matches for Canada. She led Canada in minutes played in both 2006 and 2007.

She made her international debut in a 3-1 loss to Germany at Swangard Stadium in Burnaby, then scored her first goal just three days later in a 4-3 loss to Germany at Edmonton's Commonwealth Stadium.

At the 2007 FIFA World Cup and 2008 Olympic Games, she featured in every Canada minute across both tournaments.

In club football, Franko played in both the United States and Canada. She won the WPSL Championship with the California Storm in 2002 and then the USL W-League

Championship with Vancouver Whitecaps FC in 2004 and 2006. She was the WPSL's Top Scorer in 2002.

She won the Jubilee Trophy with Surrey United SC at the National Championships in 2006 and she was the tournament's Top Scorer in both 2004 and 2006.

As a pro footballer in 2009, Franko helped the Los Angeles Sol finish first overall in the WPS standings. They finished as runners up in the playoffs after they lost the Final.

CANADA RECORDS

"A" RECORDS	MP	MS	MIN	G	A
2005 CANADA	2	2	180	1g	
2006 CANADA	17	17	1528	3g	
2007 CANADA	14	14	1260	1g	
2008 CANADA	19	18	1653		
2009 CANADA	3	3	198		
5 SEASONS	**55**	**54**	**4819**	**5g**	

FIFA / OLYMPIC	MP	MS	MIN	G	A
2007 FIFA WC	3	3	270	1g	
2008 OLYMPIC	4	4	390		

2007 FIFA WORLD CUP • Centre back Martina Franko featured in every Canada minute at the 2007 FIFA World Cup and she was up front on a set play when she scored Canada's 4-0 goal against Ghana. Franko scored on a header after a Kristina Kiss corner kick slipped through the hands of goalkeeper Memunatu Sulemana.

FORWARD

17

FABIENNE GAREAU

Born: 1967-09-20, Ottawa, ON, CAN. Grew up in Orléans, ON, CAN. Height 163 cm.

1 FIFA International Tournament: Quarterfinals at China 1988
1 Concacaf medal: Silver in 1991
1st #CANWNT: 1987-12-11 at Kaohsiung City, TPE (v. HKG)
1st Goal: 1988-06-03 at Foshan, CHN (v. CIV)

INTERNATIONAL CAREER

Fabienne Gareau represented Canada at both the World Invitational Tournament in 1987 and FIFA's International Football Tournament in 1988. She won Silver at the first Concacaf Championship in 1991.

Gareau started up front in all eight matches at the December 1987 tournament, which included two matches against club teams. She made her international debut on 11 December 1987 in a 2-0 win over Hong Kong (teammate Michele Houchen scored both goals).

In 1991, Gareau scored four goals in five matches as Canada finished second at the inaugural Concacaf Championship in Haiti. In that first year, only the Americans as Concacaf champions qualified for the FIFA World Cup. Gareau scored in the opening match against Costa Rica, then scored a hat trick in Canada's second match against Jamaica.

Across five international seasons, Gareau scored five goals in 17 career matches. She scored her first international goal against Côte d'Ivoire in 1988.

CLUB CAREER

Gareau played soccer in Canada and the United States where she was enrolled at North Carolina State University. She helped her school reach the NCAA Final in 1988 and the NCAA Semifinals in 1989.

Before enrolling at NC State, she was a two-time national champion at Canada Soccer's All-Star Championship with Ontario in 1986 and 1987.

She was named to the Atlantic Coast Conference's 50th Anniversary Women's Soccer Team in 2002.

CANADA RECORDS

"A" RECORDS		MP	MS	MIN	G	A
1987	CANADA	6	6	420		
1988	CANADA	4	4	213	1g	2a
1990	CANADA	2	2	160		1a
1991	CANADA	5	4	323	4g	
4 SEASONS		17	16	1116	5g	3a

FIFA / OLYMPIC	MP	MS	MIN	G	A
1988 FIFA	4	4	213	1g	

1988 FIFA INTERNATIONAL TOURNAMENT • Fabienne Gareau featured in all four Canada matches at FIFA's first women's international tournament in June 1988. She started all four Canada matches including the 1-0 loss to Sweden in the Quarterfinals. She scored a goal and two assists in the 6-0 win over Côte d'Ivoire.

5

ROBYN GAYLE

Born: 1985-10-31, Toronto, ON, CAN. Grew up in Mississauga, ON, CAN. Height 168 cm. Dominant right foot.

3 FIFA World Cups: China 2007, Germany 2011, Canada 2015
2 Olympic Games: Beijing 2008, Bronze at London 2012
4 Concacaf medals: Gold 2010, Silver 2006, 2008, 2012
1st #CANWNT: 2006-06-25 at Toronto, ON, CAN (v. ITA)
1st Goal: 2011-10-25 at Guadalajara, JA, MEX (v. COL)

CANADA SOCCER HALL OF FAME

Robyn Gayle represented Canada at two FIFA youth tournaments, three FIFA World Cups and two Olympic Games. She won a FIFA Silver Medal at the first FIFA U-19 World Championship in 2002, a Gold Medal at the 2011 Pan American Games, and a memorable Bronze Medal at the London 2012 Olympic Games.

From late 2010 to early 2011, she helped Canada set a program record with an 11-match undefeated streak. Inside that streak, she helped Canada win the 2010 Concacaf Championship. In 2011, she scored her first goal when she got the 2-1 match winner against Colombia in the Pan American Games Semifinals.

At the club level, Gayle played football in Canada and the United States, including the first two NWSL seasons with the Washington Spirit. She reached the NWSL Semifinals in 2014.

As a teenager, she helped Oakville SC win the Jubilee Trophy at Canada Soccer's 2002 National Championships. She later played in three USL W-League Finals, twice with Ottawa and once with Vancouver.

At the University of North Carolina, she won the 2006 NCAA College Cup and was named the Most Outstanding Defensive Player of the Tournament.

CANADA RECORDS

"A" RECORDS	MP	MS	MIN	G	A
2006 CANADA	10	6	602		
2007 CANADA	1	1	40		
2008 CANADA	14	6	615		
2009 CANADA	2	1	27		
2010 CANADA	8	2	245		
2011 CANADA	16	6	593	1g	
2012 CANADA	13	5	522	1g	
2013 CANADA	11	3	335		
2014 CANADA	5	1	169		1a
2015 CANADA	1	0	12		
10 SEASONS	**81**	**31**	**3160**	**2g**	**1a**

FIFA / OLYMPIC	MP	MS	MIN	G	A
2007 FIFA WC	0	0	0		
2008 OLYMPIC	1	0	9		
2011 FIFA WC	1	0	45		
2012 OLYMPIC	2	1	87		
2015 FIFA WC	0	0	0		

2012 OLYMPIC GAMES • Robyn Gayle made two appearances at the 2012 Olympic Football Tournament before she was ruled out through injury. With both Candace Chapman and Emily Zurrer already unavailable through injuries, Gayle switched to centre back in the second match and earned Player of the Match honours in the 3-0 win over South Africa.

MIDFIELDER

SUZANNE GERRIOR

Born: 1997-04-04, Halifax, NS, CAN. Grew up in Brookside, NS, CAN. Height 160 cm. Dominant right foot.

1 FIFA World Cup: Group phase at Sweden 1995
2 Concacaf medals: Silver in 1991 and 1994
1st #CANWNT: 1990-04-20 at Varna, BUL (v. CHN)

INTERNATIONAL CAREER

Suzanne Gerrior represented Canada at their first FIFA Women's World Cup in 1995. At age 22, she was the youngest Canadian to feature at the FIFA World Cup in Sweden.

When she made her international debut at the 1990 Varna Tournament in Bulgaria, she was in fact the second-youngest player in the five-year history of the program. Still only 17 years old, she played the second half of Canada's 2-0 loss to China PR on 20 April 1990.

Gerrior helped Canada finish in second place at both the 1991 and 1994 Concacaf Championships. While she did not feature in the 1991 tournament, she featured in Canada's last match against USA in 1994.

CLUB CAREER

Gerrior played soccer in Canada and the United States where she was enrolled at North Carolina State University. She was a First Team NSCAA Academic All-American in 1992.

Before leaving for college, Gerrior helped Dartmouth City Mazda reach the 1990 National Championships Final at Beazley Field (they lost the Jubilee Trophy to the Coquitlam Strikers).

Gerrior was honoured by the Nova Scotia Sports Hall of Fame in 2023.

CANADA RECORDS

"A" RECORDS	MP	MS	MIN	G	A
1990 CANADA	1	0	40		
1991 CANADA	0	0	0		
1994 CANADA	3	0	53		
1995 CANADA	6	1	179		
4 SEASONS	**10**	**1**	**272**		

FIFA / OLYMPIC	MP	MS	MIN	G	A
1995 FIFA WC	1	0	29		

● ● ●

1995 FIFA WORLD CUP • Suzanne Gerrior made one appearance at the FIFA Women's World Cup at Sweden 1995. She came in as a substitute for the last 29 minutes of Canada's 3-3 draw with Nigeria. It was both her first FIFA World Cup match and her last international appearance for Canada.

14

VANESSA GILLES

CENTRE BACK

Born: 1995-01-06, Châteauguay, QC, CAN. Grew up in Ottawa, ON, CAN. Height 174 cm. Dominant right foot.

1 Olympic Games: Gold at Tokyo in 2021
1 FIFA World Cup: AU NZ 2023
1 Concacaf medal: Silver in 2022
1st #CANWNT: 2019-11-10 at Yonghuan, CHN (v. NZL)
1st Goal: 2022-02-20 at Norwich, ENG (v. GER)

OLYMPIC CHAMPION

Vanessa Gilles has already represented Canada at one FIFA World Cup and one Olympic Games. She won an Olympic Gold Medal at Tokyo in 2021.

In 2021, she helped Canada set a program record with a 12-match undefeated streak. In 2022, she was a tournament all-star at the Concacaf W Championship.

Less than two years before she won an Olympic Gold Medal at Tokyo, Gilles made her international debut with Canada on 10 November 2019. She scored her first goal on 20 February 2022.

FCF OLYMPIQUE LYONNAIS

Gilles joined FCF Olympique Lyonnais in 2022-23 and won both the league title and Coupe de France. She also scored in the UEFA Champions League Quarterfinals before Lyon were eliminated on kicks.

Gilles has played her club football in Canada, Cyprus, France and USA. She won the Cyprus Cup with Apollon Limassol FC

in 2018 before she moved to France where she joined FC Girondins de Bordeaux. She played part of one season in the NWSL with Angel City FC.

Before moving to Europe, she played her college soccer at the University of Cincinnati. She played in League1 Ontario with West Ottawa SC.

CANADA RECORDS

"A" RECORDS	MP	MS	MIN	G	A
2019 CANADA	1	0	45		
2020 CANADA	1	1	90		
2021 CANADA	12	11	1050		
2022 CANADA	8	7	675	2g	
2023 CANADA	12	12	1035	1g	
FIRST 5 YEARS	34	31	2895	3g	

FIFA / OLYMPIC	MP	MS	MIN	G	A
2021 OLYMPIC	4	4	420		
2023 FIFA WC	3	3	270		

2021 OLYMPIC GAMES • Vanessa Gilles earned Player of the Match honours in back-to-back matches at the 2021 Olympic Football Tournament: both the group finale against Great Britain and the Quarterfinals against Brazil. In those Quarterfinals, she hit the crossbar in the second half, then emphatically scored on Canada's last kick in the shootout.

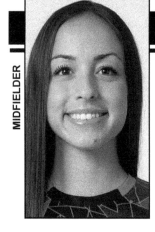

MIDFIELDER

JULIA GROSSO

Born: 2000-08-29, Vancouver, BC, CAN. Height 171 cm. Dominant left foot.

2 FIFA World Cups: France 2019, AU NZ 2023
1 Olympic Games: Gold at Tokyo in 2021
3 Concacaf medals: Silver in 2018, 2020, 2022
1st #CANWNT: 2017-11-12 at San Jose, CA, USA (v. USA)
1st Goal: 2022-07-05 FWCQ at Guadalupe, NL, MEX (v. TRI)

OLYMPIC CHAMPION

Julia Grosso has already represented Canada at one FIFA youth tournament, two FIFA World Cups and one Olympic Games. She won the Concacaf Under-15 Championship in 2014 and was the runner up in voting for Canada Soccer's Young Player award in 2018.

At Tokyo, she scored on the last kick in the shootout to capture Canada's first Olympic Gold Medal in women's football.

In 2021, she also helped Canada set a program record with a 12-match undefeated streak. The following year, she won the Golden Boot as the top scorer at the 2022 Concacaf W Championship.

In 2023, Grosso made her 50th career international appearance with Canada.

JUVENTUS FC

Grosso turned pro with Juventus FC in Italy midway through the 2021-22 season and proceeded to win the Supercoppa, the Serie A league title, and the Coppa Italia.

In 2022-23, they lost the Supercoppa and finished second in the league standings, but they again won the Coppa Italia.

Before turning pro, Grosso played college soccer at the University of Texas at Austin where she was coached by Angela Kelly, a former Canada international. Before college, she played with the Vancouver Whitecaps FC Girls Elite Program.

CANADA RECORDS

"A" RECORDS		MP	MS	MIN	G	A
2017	CANADA	1	0	1		
2018	CANADA	8	4	325		1a
2019	CANADA	7	2	188		
2020	CANADA	5	2	166		1a
2021	CANADA	10	2	455		
2022	CANADA	15	5	655	3g	1a
2023	CANADA	11	8	594		
FIRST 7 YEARS		**57**	**23**	**2384**	**3g**	**3a**

FIFA / OLYMPIC		MP	MS	MIN	G	A
2019	FIFA WC	0	0	0		
2021	OLYMPIC	5	1	246		
2023	FIFA WC	3	3	172		

● ● ●

2021 OLYMPIC GAMES • Julia Grosso made five appearances at the 2021 Olympic Football Tournament, but she will be forever remembered for her winning kick in the shootout when Canada beat Sweden for the Gold Medal. Just 20 years old at the time, Grosso beat Hedvig Lindahl with a left-footed shot on the last kick of the Final.

7

JENNY HAFTING

RIGHT BACK / F

Born: 1968-05-14, Burnaby, BC, CAN. Height 165 cm. Dominant right foot.

1 FIFA International Tournament: Quarterfinals at China 1988
1 Concacaf medal: Bronze in 1993
1st #CANWNT: 1988-06-03 at Foshan, CHN (v. CIV)

INTERNATIONAL CAREER

Jenny Hafting made her debut with Canada at FIFA's International Football Tournament in June 1988 at Foshan, China. Across six years, she made 12 international "A" appearances including a third-place finish at the 1993 Concacaf Invitational Tournament.

Along with the 1988 tournament, Hafting also took part in Canada Soccer's 1989 tour to Denmark, the 1990 Varna International Women's Tournament in Bulgaria, the 1993 Ohio Soccer Extravagenza in the United States, and the World University Games in Canada.

In 1990, she featured in Canada's first two home international matches in Winnipeg, a 2-0 loss to Norway and a 4-1 loss to the United States. In 1993, she made her last international appearance at the Concacaf tournament against champions USA.

CLUB CAREER

Hafting played her club football in Canada where she won Canada Soccer's National

Championships on two occasions. She lifted the Jubilee Trophy for the first time as a teenager in 1987 with Coquitlam United SC and then won the trophy again with Surrey Marlins SC in 1993.

Hafting was also a national runner up with Coquitlam United SC in 1988.

At the University of British Columbia, she helped her school reach the CIAU Final in 1990. She was a CIAU Second Team All-Canadian in 1990.

CANADA RECORDS

"A" RECORDS		MP	MS	MIN	G	A
1988	CANADA	3	3	240		
1989	CANADA	0	0	0		
1990	CANADA	5	4	332		
1993	CANADA	4	4	270		
1995	CANADA	0	0	0		
5 SEASONS		12	11	842		

FIFA / OLYMPIC		MP	MS	MIN	G	A
1988	FIFA WC	3	3	240		

1988 FIFA INTERNATIONAL TOURNAMENT • Jenny Hafting made three appearances for Canada at FIFA's first women's international tournament in 1988, including the narrow 1-0 loss to Sweden in the Quarterfinals. She made her international debut in the second match, a 6-0 win over Côte d'Ivoire on 3 June 1988.

FORWARD / M

12

ISABELLE HARVEY

Born: 1997-03-27, Hauterive, QC, CAN. Grew up in Cap-Rouge, QC, CAN. Height 158 cm. Dominant left foot.

1 FIFA World Cup: Group phase at USA 1999
1 Concacaf medal: Gold in 1998
1st #CANWNT: 1998-07-19 at Ottawa, ON, CAN (v. CHN)
1st Goal: 1998-08-30 FWCQ at Toronto, ON, CAN (v. MTQ)

CONCACAF CHAMPION

Isabelle Harvey represented Canada at the FIFA World Cup in 1999 after she won the Concacaf Championship in 1998. She then missed the Concacaf Gold Cup in 2000 because of school commitments.

Harvey scored her first of three international goals at the 1998 Concacaf Championship against Martinique. She later scored goals against Australia in 1999 and then Finland at the 2000 Algarve Cup.

With Canada from 1998 to 2004, Harvey made 44 international "A" appearances. She made her debut on 19 July 1998 in a 2-1 loss to China PR in Ottawa.

She made her last appearance in a 2-0 loss to the United States in Shenzhen, China on 3 February 2004.

CLUB CAREER

Harvey played her club football in Canada and USA. In 1999, she was the Soccer Québec Player of the Year (senior excellence division).

Harvey played college soccer in the United States at the University of South California. In 1998, she helped her school win their first conference championship.

She played her youth football in her home province and was named the Soccer Québec youth player of the year in 1993.

CANADA RECORDS

"A" RECORDS		MP	MS	MIN	G	A
1998	CANADA	6	1	239	1g	
1999	CANADA	11	6	662	1g	
2000	CANADA	11	10	xx	1g	
2001	CANADA	12	9	xx		
2002	CANADA	3	2	225		
2003	CANADA	0	0	0		
2004	CANADA	1	0	7		
7 SEASONS		44	28	n/a	3g	

FIFA / OLYMPIC	MP	MS	MIN	G	A
1999 FIFA WC	3	3	270		

● ● ●

1999 FIFA WORLD CUP • Isabelle Harvey featured in every Canada minute at the 1999 FIFA Women's World Cup in the United States. Canada opened the group phase with a 1-1 draw against Japan in San Jose, but then lost back-to-back matches to Norway and Russia in Washington and East Rutherford, respectively.

1

WENDY HAWTHORNE

GOALKEEPER

Born: 1960-06-07, Vancouver, BC, CAN. Height 173 cm. Dominant right foot.

1 FIFA World Cup: Group phase at Sweden 1995
3 Concacaf medals: Silver in 1991 and 1994, Bronze in 1993
1st #CANWNT: 1990-04-20 at Varna, BUL (v. CHN)
1st Clean Sheet: 1993-08-04 at Long Island, NY, USA (v. TRI)

INTERNATIONAL CAREER

Wendy Hawthorne represented Canada at their first FIFA World Cup in 1995 and won three Concacaf medals from 1991 to 1994.

She got her first call up to the National Team in April 1988, but did not travel to the FIFA International Tournament in June. She then traveled with Canada in April 1990 to the Varna Tournament in Bulgaria where she made her international "A" debut in a 2-0 loss to China PR on 20 April.

She did not feature at the 1991 Concacaf Championship in Haiti, but then played all four matches at the Concacaf Invitational Tournament in 1993. One year later, she played all four matches at the Concacaf Championship when Canada qualified for the FIFA World Cup Sweden 1995.

CLUB CAREER

Hawthorne played club football in Canada for more than two decades. She was a four-time National Championships winner for the Jubilee Trophy, winning it three successive years with the Surrey Marlins from 1991 to

1993 and then once with Vancouver UBC Alumni in 1996. She was a six-time national runner up and 11-time BC Cup provincial winner. She retired as Canada's all-time National Championships leader with 23 clean sheets in 39 matches.

In 1997, Hawthorne was a recipient of the BC Soccer Award of Merit.

CANADA RECORDS

"A" RECORDS	MP	MS	MIN		CS
1988 CANADA	0	0	0		
1990 CANADA	1	1	80	0	CS
1991 CANADA	0	0	0		
1993 CANADA	3	3	270	2	CS
1994 CANADA	9	9	810	4	CS
1995 CANADA	2	2	135	0	CS
1998 CANADA	0	0	0		
7 SEASONS	15	15	1295	6	CS

FIFA / OLYMPIC	MP	MS	MIN	CS
1995 FIFA WC	0	0	0	

FIFA WORLD CUP QUALIFIERS • Wendy Hawthorne posted three clean sheets in a row at the 1994 Concacaf Championship when Canada qualified for the FIFA Women's World Cup for the first time in program history. The following year, she was one of three goalkeepers selected to Canada's FIFA World Cup squad, but she did not feature in the tournament.

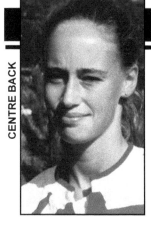

9

CENTRE BACK

JANINE HELLAND

Née Janine Wood. Born: 1990-04-24, Edmonton, AB, CAN. Height 173 cm. Dominant right foot.

2 FIFA World Cups: Group phase at Sweden 1995 and USA 1999
3 Concacaf medals: Silver in 1991 and 1994, Bronze in 1993
1st #CANWNT: 1990-04-20 at Varna, BUL (v. CHN)
1st Goal: 1996-07-04 at Rapid City, SD, USA (v. BRA)

CANADA SOCCER HALL OF FAME

Janine Helland represented Canada at two FIFA World Cups and she won three Concacaf medals from 1991 to 1994, but she missed the 1998 Concacaf Championship through injury.

She wore the captain's armband at the FIFA Women's World Cup USA 1999 and she was noted as one of Canada's outstanding players by the FIFA Technical Study Group.

Across 11 years, she made 47 international "A" appearances for Canada, at the time third most in program history.

Helland (née Wood) made her debut with Canada on their 1989 tour to Denmark with matches against local club teams. She made her international "A" debut on 20 April 1990 against China PR in Varna, Bulgaria.

At the club level, she played her football in Canada and Germany. She mostly played for the Edmonton Angels in Canada, but also played for Grün-Weiß Brauweiler in the Bundesliga (1997-98 and 1998-99).

With Edmonton, she won Canada Soccer's Jubilee Trophy in 1995 and 1999. She didn't play for the team in 2000 when she gave birth to her daughter.

With the University of Alberta, Helland lifted the Gladys Bean Memorial Trophy at the 1989 CIAU Championship. She won the Gunn Baldursson Memorial Award as the Most Valuable Player of the tournament.

CANADA RECORDS

"A" RECORDS	MP	MS	MIN	G	A
1989 CANADA					
1990 CANADA	4	4	320		
1991 CANADA	5	5	400		
1993 CANADA	5	5	450		
1994 CANADA	7	6	540		
1995 CANADA	8	8	720		
1996 CANADA	5	5	450	1g	
1997 CANADA	3	3	280		
1998 CANADA	1	1	89		
1999 CANADA	9	9	810		
10 SEASONS	**47**	**46**	**4059**	**1g**	

FIFA / OLYMPIC	MP	MS	MIN	G	A
1995 FIFA WC	3	3	270		
1999 FIFA WC	3	3	270		

● ● ●

FIFA WORLD CUPS • Janine Helland played every minute of Canada's six group matches across back-to-back FIFA World Cups at Sweden 1995 and USA 1999. She made her FIFA World Cup debut at Helsingborg in a 3-2 loss to England on 6 June, then helped Canada get their first point in a 3-3 draw with Nigeria just two days later.

23

JENNA HELLSTROM

WINGER / FB

Born: 1995-04-21, Sudbury, ON, CAN. Height 168 cm. Dominant right foot.

1 FIFA World Cup: Round of 16 at France 2019
1st #CANWNT: 2018-03-05 at Lagos, POR (v. KOR)

INTERNATIONAL CAREER

Jenna Hellstrom represented Canada at the FIFA World Cup in 2019 and helped the squad reach the Round of 16. One of the fastest players in the squad, she was capable at playing either as a winger or as an outside fullback.

After making her international debut in 2018, she made another three international "A" appearances in 2019. She made her debut at the 2018 Algarve Cup in a 3-0 win over Korea Republic.

With Head Coach Bev Priestman, Hellstrom featured against Mexico in 2021 and then made her final appearance against USA in February 2023. In all, she made seven career appearances from 2017 to 2023.

CLUB CAREER

Hellstrom played her club football in Canada, Sweden, USA and France. She spent her last professional season with Dijon FCO in the Championnat de France. She scored her last professional goal on 21 January 2023.

Hellstrom notably kicked off her pro career with second-place FC Rosengård in the Swedish Damallsvenskan in 2017. While she didn't win the league, she did win the domestic cup (Svenska Cupen). She also made her UEFA Champions League debut in the Round of 16.

Before turning pro, she played her college soccer at Kent University. She played her youth soccer in Sudbury.

CANADA RECORDS

"A" RECORDS	MP	MS	MIN	G	A
2017 CANADA	0	0	0		
2018 CANADA	1	1	60		
2019 CANADA	3	0	40		1a
2020 CANADA	0	0	0		
2021 CANADA	1	0	11		
2023 CANADA	1	0	45		
6 SEASONS	7	1	156		1a

FIFA / OLYMPIC	MP	MS	MIN	G	A
2019 FIFA WC	0	0	0		

1st INTERNATIONAL ASSIST • Jenna Hellstrom got her first international assist in the build up to the 2019 FIFA Women's World Cup France 2019. In Canada's first international match of the year, she delivered the cross for Christine Sinclair's 1-0 match winner against Norway. Hellstrom got the assist less than five minutes after she entered the match as a substitute.

CENTRE BACK / M

11

RANDEE HERMUS

Born: 1979-11-14, Langley, BC, CAN. Height 173 cm. Dominant right foot.

2 FIFA World Cups: 4th Place in 2003, Group phase in 2007
1 Olympic Games: Quarterfinals at Beijing 2008
4 Concacaf medals: Silver 2002, 2006, 2008, Bronze 2004
1st #CANWNT: 2000-03-12 at Lagoa, POR (v. CHN)
1st Goal: 2002-03-05 Silves, POR (v. POR)

CANADA SOCCER HALL OF FAME

Randee Hermus represented Canada at two FIFA World Cups and the Beijing 2008 Olympic Games. She won four Concacaf medals and captured Bronze at the 2007 Pan American Games in Brazil. When she left international football, she ranked fourth all time with 113 appearances for Canada. She scored 12 goals across her career.

She set a Canada record by featuring in 46 consecutive international matches from 2005 to 2008. She was Canada's 2005 leader in minutes played and she finished second to Christine Sinclair in Player of the Year voting in both 2005 and 2006.

While Hermus helped Canada finish in fourth place at the 2003 FIFA World Cup, she was unable to play because of an injury. Four years later, she played every Canada minute at the 2007 FIFA World Cup.

In 2008, Hermus made her Olympic debut in Canada's 1-1 draw with hosts China PR in front of 52,600 fans, the largest crowd in front of which Canada had ever played.

Hermus played her club football in Canada and Norway. She led Vancouver Whitecaps FC to the USL W-League Championship in 2004 and 2006 and she won MVP honours in 2004. With Surrey United SC, she won the Jubilee Trophy in 2006 and 2011. At the Canada Games, she won a Gold Medal in 1997 with British Columbia.

CANADA RECORDS

"A" RECORDS	MP	MS	MIN	G	A
1998 CANADA	0	0	0		
2000 CANADA	12	9	759		
2001 CANADA	8	3	xx		1a
2002 CANADA	12	12	1039	2g	
2003 CANADA	12	12	973	2g	
2004 CANADA	9	9	769		1a
2005 CANADA	10	10	900	1g	
2006 CANADA	17	16	1409	3g	
2007 CANADA	14	14	1235	2g	
2008 CANADA	19	17	1463	2g	1a
10 SEASONS	113	102	n/a	12g	3a

FIFA / OLYMPIC	MP	MS	MIN	G	A
2003 FIFA WC	INJ	0	0		
2007 FIFA WC	3	3	270		
2008 OLYMPIC	1	1	64		

● ● ●

2007 FIFA WORLD CUP • Randee Hermus made her FIFA World Cup debut in 2007 when she featured in every Canada minute across the group phase in China. Canada lost 2-1 to Norway in their opener, won 4-0 over Ghana in their second match, but were ultimately eliminated after a 2-2 draw with Australia in their third match.

10

FORWARD / CB

CHARMAINE HOOPER

Born: 1968-01-15, Georgetown, GUY. Grew up in Ottawa, ON, CAN. Height 170 cm. Dominant left foot.

3 FIFA World Cups: Group phase in 1995, 1999, 4th Place in 2003
6 Concacaf: Gold 1998, Silver 1991, 1994, 2002, Bronze 1993, 2004
1st #CANWNT: 1986-07-07 at Blaine, MN, USA (v. USA)
1st Goal: 1991-04-16 FWCQ at Port-au-Prince, HAI (v. CRC)

CANADA SOCCER HALL OF FAME

Charmaine Hooper represented Canada at three FIFA World Cups including a fourth-place finish at USA 2003. One of Canada's original Women's National Team players in 1986, she retired as Canada's all-time leader in appearances (129) and goals scored (71).

She won the Concacaf Championship in 1998 and helped Canada set a program record with a 10-match undefeated streak in 2003. She was also a four-time Canada Soccer Player of the Year after the award was inaugurated in 1994 (she won that award in 1994, 1995, 2002 and 2003).

She set a Canada record with seven goals in 1991 and then broke her own record with 10 goals scored in 1994. She scored her 50th career goal on 30 October 2002 when she scored a hat trick against Haiti.

Hooper played her club football in Canada, USA, Norway, Italy and Japan. She helped Prima Ham FC Kunoichi win Japan's 1995 L.League title and then the Chicago Cobras win the 2000 USL W-League Championship. She reached the WUSA Final in both 2001 and 2003 with the Atlanta Beat.

CANADA RECORDS

"A" RECORDS	MP	MS	MIN	G	A
1986 CANADA	2	2	180		1a
1987 CANADA	3	2	xx		
1990 CANADA	2	2	xx		
1991 CANADA	5	5	400	7g	
1993 CANADA	6	6	540	1g	
1994 CANADA	11	11	990	10g	1a
1995 CANADA	11	11	938	4g	3a
1998 CANADA	8	8	632	6g	1a
1999 CANADA	11	11	969	8g	2a
2000 CANADA	7	6	585	8g	2a
2001 CANADA	11	11	899	4g	
2002 CANADA	11	11	942	8g	2a
2003 CANADA	17	16	1391	4g	4a
2004 CANADA	10	10	823	2g	1a
2005 CANADA	7	3	282	2g	2a
2006 CANADA	7	7	556	7g	
16 SEASONS	**129**	**122**	**n/a**	**71g**	**19a**

FIFA / OLYMPIC	MP	MS	MIN	G	A
1995 FIFA WC	3	3	270		2a
1999 FIFA WC	3	3	270	2g	
2003 FIFA WC	6	6	540	2g	1a

FIFA WORLD CUPS • Charmaine Hooper played every Canada minute across three FIFA World Cups from Sweden 1995 to a fourth-place finish at USA 2003. In her third FIFA World Cup, she wore the captain's armband and was named to the team's all-star tournament. She famously scored the 1-0 match winner against China PR in the Quarterfinals.

FORWARD

JORDYN HUITEMA

Born: 2001-05-08, Chilliwack, BC, CAN. Height 181 cm. Dominant right foot.

2 FIFA World Cups: France 2019, AU NZ 2023
1 Olympic Games: Gold at Tokyo in 2021
3 Concacaf medals: Silver in 2018, 2020, 2022
1st #CANWNT: 2017-03-08 at São João da Venda, POR (v. ESP)
1st Goal: 2017-06-11 at Toronto, ON, CAN (v. CRC)

OLYMPIC CHAMPION

Jordyn Huitema has already represented Canada at two FIFA youth tournaments, two FIFA World Cups and one Olympic Games. She won the Concacaf Under-15 Championship in 2014 and the Canada Soccer Young Player award in 2018.

In 2021, she won an Olympic Gold Medal with Canada. She also helped Canada set a program record with a 12-match undefeated streak.

Huitema was just 16 years old when she scored her first two international goals at Toronto in 2017.

In 2019, she made her FIFA World Cup debut in the third group match at Reims against the Netherlands.

In 2020, Huitema led Canada with seven goals, including five goals in a win over Jamaica. She scored the match winner that qualified Canada for the Tokyo Olympic Games.

In 2022, she led Canada with five assists in 15 international matches.

SEATTLE REIGN FC

In her first NWSL season, Huitema helped OL Reign FC win the 2022 NWSL Shield. She previously played three pro seasons in France with Paris Saint-Germain FC where she won the league title in 2020-21 and the Coupe de France in 2022.

Before moving overseas, she played with the Vancouver Whitecaps FC Girls Elite Program.

CANADA RECORDS

"A" RECORDS	MP	MS	MIN	G	A
2017 CANADA	7	1	113	2g	
2018 CANADA	8	2	232	4g	
2019 CANADA	10	6	564		
2020 CANADA	8	3	380	7g	1a
2021 CANADA	12	1	409	1g	
2022 CANADA	15	8	756	1g	5a
2023 CANADA	13	6	695	3g	
FIRST 7 YEARS	73	27	3149	18g	6a

FIFA / OLYMPIC	MP	MS	MIN	G	A
2019 FIFA WC	1	1	90		
2021 OLYMPIC	4	0	88		
2023 FIFA WC	3	3	225		

● ● ●

2021 OLYMPIC GAMES • Jordyn Huitema made four appearances at the Olympic Football Tournament in 2021 when Canada captured their historic Gold Medal. Still just 20 years old and the youngest player in the Canada squad, she featured as a substitute in all three knockout matches including the Final against Sweden.

18

MIDFIELDER / F

SELENIA IACCHELLI

Born: 1986-06-05, Edmonton, AB, CAN. Height 173 cm. Dominant right foot.

1 FIFA World Cup: Quarterfinals at Canada 2015
1st #CANWNT: 2013-11-24 at Vancouver, BC, CAN (v. MEX)

INTERNATIONAL CAREER

Selenia Iacchelli represented Canada at two FIFA youth tournaments and one FIFA World Cup. She also won a Silver Medal at the Pan American Games in 2003.

Iacchelli got call ups to the National Team with coach Even Pellerud in 2005 and coach Carolina Morace in 2010, but neither camp featured an international match.

Iacchelli then got called up by coach John Herdman and she made her international debut on 24 November 2013. In all, she featured as a sub three times late that year and once again in November 2014.

At the 2003 Pan American Games with the U-23 team, she came off the bench in the Final with Canada trailing 1-0. Canada equalised on a Kristina Kiss free kick, but then lost the Final in extra time when Cristiane scored her golden goal.

CLUB CAREER

Iacchelli played her club football in Canada, USA and Italy. With Edmonton Victoria SC,

she won the Jubilee Trophy at Canada Soccer's 2013 National Championships.

It Italy, she won the 2009-10 Serie A title with ASD Torres.

Iacchelli played her college soccer at the University of Nebraska. She was a three-time First Team Academic All-Big 12 selection from 2006 to 2008.

As a teen, she helped Alberta's U-17 team win a youth all-star championship in 2003.

CANADA RECORDS

"A" RECORDS	MP	MS	MIN	G	A
2005 CANADA	0	0	0		
2010 CANADA	0	0	0		
2013 CANADA	3	0	15		
2014 CANADA	1	0	22		1a
2015 CANADA	0	0	0		
5 SEASONS	4	0	37		1a

FIFA / OLYMPIC	MP	MS	MIN	G	A
2015 FIFA WC	0	0	0		

1st INTERNATIONAL ASSIST • Selenia Iacchelli recorded her first international assist when she set up Christine Sinclair for Canada's 1-1 equaliser against Sweden in November 2014. At the time, it was just her fourth international appearance. Less than six months later, she was selected to the Canada squad for their home FIFA World Cup in June 2015.

CENTRE BACK / M

14

SARAH JOLY

Born: 1977-02-16, Lethbridge, AB, CAN. Height 168 cm. Dominant right foot.

1 FIFA World Cup: Group phase at USA 1999
1 Concacaf medal: Gold in 1998
1st #CANWNT: 1996-07-04 at Rapid City, SD, USA (v. BRA)
1st Goal: 1999-05-24 at Burnaby, BC, CAN (v. MEX)

CONCACAF CHAMPION

Sarah Joly represented Canada at the 1999 FIFA World Cup after winning the Concacaf Championship in 1998. She played in every minute of the Concacaf Championship as Canada posted five consecutive clean sheets. They won 1-0 over Mexico in the Final at Centennial Stadium in Toronto.

In 1998, she was the only player that featured in every minute of Canada's eight international matches. Predominantly a midfielder, she slipped back to play centre back at the 1998 Concacaf Championship to cover for injured captain Janine Helland.

Across five years, Joly played 17 matches for Canada at the international "A" level. She played her last international match on 6 June 1999 in Portland against the United States.

CLUB CAREER

Joly played her club football in Canada and won the 1999 Jubilee Trophy at Canada Soccer's National Championships with the Edmonton Angels. She previously won a runners up medal with her hometown Lethbridge Chargers at the 1994 National Championships.

She also played at the University of Alberta where she played for coach Tracy David, a former Canada international. Together, they lifted the Gladys Bean Memorial Trophy as national champions in 1997, then finished as runners up two years later in 1999. Joly also won the Chantal Navert Memorial Award as the CIAU's top player in 1998.

CANADA RECORDS

"A" RECORDS	MP	MS	MIN	G	A
1996 CANADA	2	1	118		
1997 CANADA	2	1	91		
1998 CANADA	8	8	720		
1999 CANADA	5	3	297	1g	
2000 CANADA	0	0	0		
5 SEASONS	17	13	1226	1g	

FIFA / OLYMPIC	MP	MS	MIN	G	A
1999 FIFA WC	0	0	0		

● ● ●

1st INTERNATIONAL GOAL • Sarah Joly scored her first international goal in a 1999 home international friendly match at Swangard Stadium in Burnaby, British Columbia. Playing at midfield, she scored Canada's 2-0 goal late in the first half as Canada beat Mexico for the second time in four days.

15

CHRISTINA JULIEN

FORWARD

Born: 1988-05-06, Cornwall, ON, CAN. Grew up in William-stown, ON, CAN. Height 167 cm. Dominant left foot.

1 FIFA World Cup: Group phase at Germany 2011
1 Olympic Games: Bronze at London 2012
2 Concacaf medals: Gold in 2010, Silver in 2012
1st #CANWNT: 2009-03-05 at Paralimni, CYP (v. NZL)
1st Goal: 2009-03-05 at Paralimni, CYP (v. NZL)

CONCACAF CHAMPION

Christina Julien represented Canada at one FIFA World Cup and she was an alternate at London 2012 when Canada won a historic Bronze Medal. She helped Canada win the 2010 Concacaf Championship and the 2011 Pan American Games.

Julien lifted her first title at the 2010 Cyprus Cup when she led Canada with three goals in four matches. Later that year, she helped Canada establish a program record with an 11-match undefeated streak through to January 2011. In that streak, she won trophies at the Concacaf Championship and Torneio Internacional.

In 2011, Julien won the Cyprus Cup in March, made her FIFA World Cup debut in June, and won the Pan American Games Gold Medal in November.

From 2009 to 2015, Julien made 54 career international appearances with Canada. She was 20 years old when she scored in her Canada debut on 5 March 2009 at the Cyprus Cup. Starting up front alongside Christine Sinclair, Julien scored the first goal in a 1-1 draw with New Zealand.

CLUB CAREER

Julien played club football in Canada, USA, Sweden, Russia, Germany and Australia. In 2013, she was the first Canadian to feature in the UEFA Women's Champions League knockout phase. In Canada, she reached the USL W-League Final in both 2010 with Ottawa Fury FC and 2013 with the Comètes de Laval.

She was honoured by the James Madison University Athletics Hall of Fame.

CANADA RECORDS

"A" RECORDS		MP	MS	MIN	G	A
2009	CANADA	4	3	187	1g	1a
2010	CANADA	14	9	754	4g	1a
2011	CANADA	20	10	944	4g	
2012	CANADA	10	8	652	1g	1a
2013	CANADA	4	0	110		
2014	CANADA	0	0	0		
2015	CANADA	2	0	17		
7 SEASONS		54	30	2664	10g	3a

FIFA / OLYMPIC		MP	MS	MIN	G	A
2011	FIFA WC	2	1	94		
2012	OLYMPIC	-	-	-		

2011 PAN AMERICAN GAMES • Christina Julien played in all five Canada matches when they won a Gold Medal at the Pan American Games Guadalajara 2011. She scored two goals in the tournament: the opening goal in a 3-1 win over Costa Rica; and then the 1-0 match winner over Argentina just two days later.

MIDFIELDER

ANGELA KELLY

Born: 1971-10-03, Glasgow, SCO. Grew up in Brantford, ON, CAN. Height 160 cm. Dominant right foot.

1 FIFA World Cup: Group phase at Sweden 1995
2 Concacaf medals: Silver in 1994, Bronze in 1993
1st #CANWNT: 1990-04-16 at Varna, BUL (v. URS)
1st Goal: 1990-04-21 at Varna, BUL (v. URS)

CANADA SOCCER HALL OF FAME

Angela Kelly represented Canada at their first FIFA World Cup in 1995. It marked the culmination of her six-year career with Canada. She left international football ranked tied for eighth all time with 29 career international "A" appearances for Canada.

Kelly played in nearly every minute of each major tournament with Canada. In 1993, she helped Canada finish in fifth place at the World University Games in Hamilton, then won Bronze at the Concacaf Invitational Tournament in New York.

In 1994, she played all but three minutes at the Concacaf Championship in Montréal when Canada qualified for the 1995 FIFA World Cup.

At the club level, Kelly played her football in Canada and the United States. She notably helped the Raleigh Wings win the USL W-League Championship.

In college, she played for the University of North Carolina. She led her school to four-straight NCAA College Cup titles from 1991 to 1994. She was a First Team All-American in 1994.

At the youth level, Kelly helped Burlington win Canada Soccer's U-18 Cup in 1988.

CANADA RECORDS

"A" RECORDS	MP	MS	MIN	G	A
1990 CANADA	3	2	93	1g	
1993 CANADA	4	3	315		
1994 CANADA	11	8	794		
1995 CANADA	11	11	941		2a
4 SEASONS	**29**	**24**	**2143**	**1g**	**2a**

FIFA / OLYMPIC	MP	MS	MIN	G	A
1995 FIFA WC	3	3	270		

● ● ●

1995 FIFA WORLD CUP • Angela Kelly played in every minute of Canada's three group matches at the 1995 FIFA World Cup in Sweden. In Canada's first two matches, she initiated the plays that led to goals against England (scored by Geri Donnelly) and Nigeria (scored by Silvana Burtini), both times initiated with her throws from the sideline.

MIDFIELDER / FB

KRISTINA KISS

Born: 1981-02-13, Ottawa, ON, CAN. Grew up in Kanata, ON, CAN. Height 163 cm. Dominant right foot.

2 FIFA World Cups: 4th Place in 2003, Group phase in 2007
3 Concacaf medals: Silver in 2002, 2006, 2008
1st #CANWNT: 2000-03-12 at Lagoa, POR (v. CHN)
1st Goal: 2000-05-31 at Canberra, AUS (v. NZL)

INTERNATIONAL CAREER

Kristina Kiss represented Canada at two FIFA World Cups including a fourth-place finish at USA 2003. She led Canada's U-23 squad to a Silver Medal at the 2003 Pan American Games in Santo Domingo.

Kiss captained Canada at the 2003 Pan American Games and she was Canada's top scorer. She got the 1-1 equaliser on a direct free kick in the Final before Brazil's Cristiane scored the 2-1 golden goal match winner in extra time.

In 2007, Kiss helped the full National Team win a Bronze Medal at the Pan American Games in Rio.

From 2000 to 2008, Kiss made 75 career international "A" appearances. She was 19 years old when she made her debut in a 4-0 loss to China at the Algarve Cup.

CLUB CAREER

Kiss played her club football in Canada and Norway. As a teenager, she helped Nepean United lift the Jubilee Trophy at Canada Soccer's 1998 National Championships. She led her team with four goals at the 1998 tournament and then again with four goals at the 1999 tournament when they finished in third place.

After her move to Norway, she helped IF Fløya earn promotion to the Toppserien in 2002 and then finish fourth overall in 2004.

In 2015, she was honoured by the Ottawa Sports Hall of Fame.

CANADA RECORDS

"A" RECORDS	MP	MS	MIN	G	A
2000 CANADA	16	12	xx	2g	2a
2001 CANADA	11	7	802	3g	3a
2002 CANADA	5	0	85		2a
2003 CANADA	18	14	1174		3a
2006 CANADA	7	5	385		1a
2007 CANADA	12	10	881	2g	1a
2008 CANADA	6	3	254	1g	
7 SEASONS	75	51	n/a	8g	12a

FIFA / OLYMPIC	MP	MS	MIN	G	A
2003 FIFA WC	6	3	319		1a
2007 FIFA WC	2	2	180		

2003 FIFA WORLD CUP • Kristina Kiss represented Canada at back-to-back FIFA World Cups at USA 2003 and China 2007. Just five weeks after the 2003 Pan American Games, she featured in all six FIFA World Cup matches. In the opener against Germany, she delivered the free kick from which Christine Sinclair scored her first career FIFA World Cup goal.

MIDFIELDER

KAYLYN KYLE

Born: 1988-10-06, Saskatoon, SK, CAN. Height 173 cm. Dominant right foot.

2 FIFA World Cups: Group phase in 2011, Quarterfinals in 2015
1 Olympic Games: Bronze at London 2012
2 Concacaf medals: Gold in 2010, Silver in 2012
1st #CANWNT: 2008-01-16 at Guangzhou, CHN (v. USA)
1st Goal: 2011-05-15 at Roma, ITA (v. SUI)

OLYMPIC BRONZE MEDAL

Kaylyn Kyle represented Canada at two FIFA youth tournaments, two FIFA World Cups and one Olympic Games. She won won the Concacaf Under-20 Championship in 2008 and the Concacaf Championship in 2010. She won a Bronze Medal at the London 2012 Olympic Games.

From late 2010 to early 2011, Kyle helped Canada set a program record with an 11-match undefeated streak. From 2011 to 2014, she played in 62 straight Canada matches.

Kyle started all three matches at her first FIFA World Cup in 2011. Four years later, she featured in all five Canada matches as they reached the Quarterfinals at Canada 2015. In the Round of 16, she made her 100th career appearance.

CLUB CAREER

Kyle played her club football in Canada, Sweden and the United States. In 2010, she helped Vancouver Whitecaps FC reach the USL W-League Final. From 2013 to 2016,

she was one of three Canadians that played more than 5,000 minutes in the NWSL's first four seasons.

Kyle turned pro in Sweden on 1 April 2009 with Piteå IF. She played her college soccer at the University of Saskatchewan and she won Canada Soccer's National Championships with Surrey United SC.

CANADA RECORDS

"A" RECORDS		MP	MS	MIN	G	A
2008	CANADA	5	2	179		1a
2009	CANADA	5	4	327		
2010	CANADA	10	9	745		1a
2011	CANADA	23	21	1531	3g	3a
2012	CANADA	22	9	1046	1g	
2013	CANADA	17	8	938	1g	1a
2014	CANADA	10	6	562	1g	
2015	CANADA	9	2	288		
8 SEASONS		101	61	5616	6g	5a

FIFA / OLYMPIC		MP	MS	MIN	G	A
2011	FIFA WC	3	3	183		
2012	OLYMPIC	6	2	282		
2015	FIFA WC	5	1	144		

● ● ●

2012 OLYMPIC GAMES • Kaylyn Kyle featured in all six matches when Canada won their inspiring Bronze Medal at the Olympic Football Tournament in 2012. In their win over South Africa, she was part of the build up on Christine Sinclair's second goal. In the their win over France, she was part of the attack when Diana Matheson scored her heroic match winner.

GOALKEEPER

STEPHANIE LABBÉ

Born: 1986-10-10, Edmonton, AB, CAN. Grew up in Stony Plain, AB, CAN. Height 175 cm. Dominant left right.

3 FIFA World Cups: Germany 2011, Canada 2015, France 2019
2 Olympic Games: Bronze at Rio 2016, Gold at Tokyo in 2021
4 Concacaf medals: Gold in 2010 Silver in 2016, 2018, 2020
1st #CANWNT: 2008-07-27 at Singapore, SIN (v SIN)
1st Clean Sheet: 2010-10-31 FWCQ at Cancún, QR, MEX (v GUY)

OLYMPIC CHAMPION

Stephanie Labbé represented Canada at two FIFA youth tournaments, three FIFA World Cups and two Olympic Games. For her 2020-21 season, she finished second in voting for the The Best FIFA Women's Goalkeeper award.

She won an Olympic Bronze Medal in 2016 and an Olympic Gold Medal in 2021. She won the Concacaf Championship in 2010.

From 2004 to 2022, Labbé made 86 career international appearances for Canada. She was just 21 years old when she made her debut before the 2008 Olympic Games in Singapore.

In 2022, she played her last international match at BC Place in Vancouver. She retired ranked third all time in Canada clean sheets, just one back of Erin McLeod and two back of Karina LeBlanc.

Across her career, Labbé played her club football in Canada, USA, Sweden and France. She won the NWSL Shield and NWSL Championship in 2019 with the North Carolina Courage.

She was 22 years old when she made her pro debut with Piteå IF on 1 April 2009. She later played in UEFA Champions League with Linköpings FC, FC Rosengård and Paris Saint-Germain FC.

CANADA RECORDS

"A" RECORDS		MP	MS	MIN		CS
2004	CANADA	0	0	0		
2008	CANADA	1	0	35	0	CS
2009	CANADA	0	0	0		
2010	CANADA	4	4	360	3	CS
2011	CANADA	4	2	256	3	CS
2012	CANADA	1	1	90	0	CS
2013	CANADA	3	1	180	2	CS
2014	CANADA	3	3	270	0	CS
2015	CANADA	7	6	550	3	CS
2016	CANADA	14	14	1215	6	CS
2017	CANADA	10	9	765	3	CS
2018	CANADA	9	9	810	4	CS
2019	CANADA	11	11	990	8	CS
2020	CANADA	5	5	450	3	CS
2021	CANADA	13	12	1101	9	CS
2022	CANADA	1	1	47	1	CS
16 SEASONS		**86**	**78**	**7119**	**45**	**CS**

FIFA / OLYMPIC		MP	MS	MIN		CS
2011	FIFA WC	0	0	0		
2015	FIFA WC	0	0	0		
2016	OLYMPIC	5	5	450	2	CS
2019	FIFA WC	4	4	360	2	CS
2021	OLYMPIC	5	5	478	3	CS

2021 OLYMPIC GAMES • Stephanie Labbé was the hero of the 2021 Olympic Football Tournament when Canada captured a historic Gold Medal in Japan. In shootouts against Brazil and Sweden, she made two saves each time: she stopped Andressa and Rafaelle in the Quarterfinals; she then stopped Anna Anvegård and Jonna Andersson in the Final.

FORWARD

20

CLOÉ LACASSE

Born: 1993-07-07, Sudbury, ON, CAN. Height 170 cm. Dominant right foot.

1 FIFA World Cup: AU NZ 2023
1 Concacaf medal: Silver in 2022
1st #CANWNT: 2021-11-27 at Ciudad México, DF, MEX (v. MEX)
1st Goal: 2022-10-06 at Sanlúcar de Barrameda, ESP (v. ARG)

INTERNATIONAL CAREER

Cloé Lacasse represented Canada at the FIFA Women's World Cup Australia & New Zealand 2023.

On 27 November 2021 just a few months after the Olympic Games, Lacasse made her international debut against Mexico. She came in as a substitute and earned Canada's Player of the Match honours.

In 2022, she won Silver at the Concacaf W Championship as Canada qualified for the 2023 FIFA World Cup. She featured in group wins over both Panama and Costa Rica. She then scored her first international goal on 6 October 2022 in a 2-0 win over Argentina.

ARSENAL FC

Lacasse joined Arsenal FC ahead of the 2023-24 season and she won the League Cup in March 2024.

In Portugal, she played four seasons with Benfica and won three-straight league titles after the global pandemic. In 2022-23, she

was named the league's Best Player as Benfica had their best season with 21 wins and just one loss in 22 league matches.

Across her four seasons, she also won the League Cup three times (Taça da Ligua) and the Supercup twice (Supertaça).

So far, Lacasse has played her club football in Canada, USA, Iceland and Portugal. With Vestmannaeyja, she won the Iceland Cup in 2017.

Before moving overseas, she played her college soccer at the University of Iowa. She played her youth soccer in Sudbury.

CANADA RECORDS

"A" RECORDS	MP	MS	MIN	G	A
2021 CANADA	2	0	59		
2022 CANADA	13	3	406	1g	
2023 CANADA	13	6	692	2g	1a
FIRST 3 YEARS	28	9	1157	3g	1a

FIFA / OLYMPIC	MP	MS	MIN	G	A
2023 FIFA WC	3	0	121		

2023 FIFA WORLD CUP • Cloé Lacasse featured in all three Canada matches at the FIFA Women's World Cup Australia & New Zealand 2023. After a 0-0 draw with Nigeria and a 2-1 win over the Republic of Ireland, Canada were eliminated after a 4-0 loss to Australia. Coming off the bench, Lacasse ranked third on Canada with six crosses.

15

FORWARD / M

KARA LANG

Born: 1986-10-22, Calgary, AB, CAN. Grew up in Oakville, ON, CAN. Height 178 cm. Dominant right foot.

2 FIFA World Cups: 4th Place in 2003, Group phase in 2007
1 Olympic Games: Quarterfinals at Beijing 2008
4 Concacaf medals: Gold 2010, Silver 2002, 2008, Bronze 2004
1st #CANWNT: 2002-03-01 at Quarteira, POR (v. SCO)
1st Goal: 2002-03-03 at Lagoa, POR (v. WAL)

CANADA SOCCER HALL OF FAME

Kara Lang represented Canada at two FIFA World Cups and one Olympic Games as an international footballer. Canada's youngest debutant at age 15, she played 92 times for Canada before retiring through injuries at age 24.

She made her last appearance at the 2010 Concacaf Championship when Canada lifted the confederation title for the second time in program history.

Lang won a Silver Medal from the first FIFA U-19 World Championship in 2002. She won the Concacaf Under-19 Championship in 2004.

She twice helped Canada set program records for unbeaten streaks (2003 and 2010-11). She made her FIFA World Cup debut and was Canada's joint top scorer in 2003.

When she retired again after her attempted comeback, she still ranked fourth all time with 34 career goals for Canada.

Lang played her club football in Canada and the United States. She helped Vancouver Whitecaps FC win the 2004 USL W-League Championship, but missed their 2006 title weekend through injury.

CANADA RECORDS

"A" RECORDS	MP	MS	MIN	G	A
2002 CANADA	15	11	1136	10g	2a
2003 CANADA	21	21	1740	11g	3a
2004 CANADA	7	4	364		
2005 CANADA	7	5	477	2g	
2006 CANADA	3	0	78		
2007 CANADA	13	10	771	4g	4a
2008 CANADA	19	16	1481	6g	1a
2009 CANADA	3	3	260		
2010 CANADA	4	1	128	1g	1a
2013 CANADA	0	0	0		
2014 CANADA	0	0	0		
11 SEASONS	92	71	6435	34g	11a

FIFA / OLYMPIC	MP	MS	MIN	G	A
2003 FIFA WC	6	6	489	2g	1a
2007 FIFA WC	3	3	235		3a
2008 OLYMPIC	4	4	389	1g	1a

FIFA WORLD CUPS • Kara Lang was one of the youngest players at USA 2003 when she made her FIFA World Cup debut with Canada. She scored two goals in the tournament: the 3-1 goal against Japan in the group phase; and the opening goal of the Semifinals before Canada lost 2-1 to Sweden.

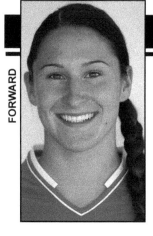

FORWARD

2

CHRISTINE LATHAM

Born: 1981-09-15, Calgary, AB, CAN. Height 173 cm.

1 FIFA World Cup: 4th Place at USA 2003
1 Concacaf medal: Bronze in 2004
1st #CANWNT: 2000-05-05 at Portland, OR, USA (v. KOR)
1st Goal: 2000-06-10 at Newcastle, AUS (v. JPN)

INTERNATIONAL CAREER

Christine Latham represented Canada at the 2003 FIFA World Cup in the United States. Canada finished in fourth place, still the nation's best finish at a FIFA World Cup.

In her first two seasons with the National Team, she scored five goals in 18 matches and helped Canada finish in fourth place at the 2000 Concacaf Gold Cup.

In the build up to the FIFA World Cup in 2003, she helped Canada set a program record with a 10-match undefeated streak.

From 2000 to 2006, she made 49 career international "A" appearances for Canada. She was just 18 years old when she made her debut on 5 May 2000 in a 1-0 win over Korea Republic.

CLUB CAREER

Latham played her club football in Canada and the United States. In 2003, she helped the San Diego Spirit finish third in the WUSA standings and reach the playoffs. She was named the league's Rookie of the Year.

Latham played her college soccer at the University of Nebraska. She was a MAC Hermann Trophy Award Finalist in 2001 and 2002.

At the youth level, she played for Calgary Celtic SFC where she won Canada Soccer's U-17 Cup in 1998. She also helped Alberta's U-18 team win a youth all-star championship that same year.

She was honoured by the University of Nebraska Athletics Hall of Fame in 2015.

CANADA RECORDS

"A" RECORDS	MP	MS	MIN	G	A
2000 CANADA	12	10	xx	4g	1a
2001 CANADA	6	6	495	1g	
2003 CANADA	17	17	1191	7g	5a
2004 CANADA	5	5	439	3g	1a
2005 CANADA	3	0	86		
2006 CANADA	6	5	495		
6 SEASONS	49	43	n/a	15g	7a

FIFA / OLYMPIC	MP	MS	MIN	G	A
2003 FIFA WC	6	6	470	3g	1a

2003 FIFA WORLD CUP • Christine Latham co-led Canada with three goals in six matches at the FIFA Women's World Cup USA 2003. In the group phase, she scored two goals in the 3-0 win over Argentina and then one goal in the 3-1 win over Japan. In Canada's last match of the tournament, she got an assist on Christine Sinclair's goal against USA.

10

ASHLEY LAWRENCE

FULLBACK / M

Born: 1995-06-11, Toronto, ON, CAN. Grew up in Caledon East, ON, CAN. Height 170 cm. Dominant right foot.

3 FIFA World Cups: Canada 2015, France 2019, AU NZ 2023
2 Olympic Games: Bronze at Rio 2016, Gold at Tokyo in 2021
4 Concacaf medals: Silver in 2016, 2018, 2020, 2022
1st #CANWNT: 2013-01-12 at Yongchuan, CHN (v. CHN)
1st Goal: 2015-06-15 FWC at Montréal, QC, CAN (v. NED)

OLYMPIC CHAMPION

Ashley Lawrence has already represented Canada at three FIFA youth tournaments, three FIFA World Cups and two Olympic Games. She won the U-17 Player of the Year award in 2011 and 2012, then won Canada Soccer's Player of the Year award for the first time in 2019.

She won an Olympic Bronze Medal in 2016 and an Olympic Gold Medal in 2021. She also helped Canada set a program record with a 12-match undefeated streak.

At her first FIFA World Cup in 2015, she scored the opening goal of Canada's 1-1 draw with Netherlands at Montréal. From 2015 to 2023, she started all 12 Canada matches including the Quarterfinals in 2015.

In February 2024, she was named to the Best XI at the Concacaf W Gold Cup.

CHELSEA FC

Ashley Lawrence joined Chelsea FC ahead of the 2023-24 season. They were runners up in the 2024 League Cup.

A UEFA Champions League runner up in 2016-17 with Paris Saint-Germain FC, she was a Championnat de France winner (2020-21) and two-time Coupe de France winner (2018, 2022).

CANADA RECORDS

"A" RECORDS	MP	MS	MIN	G	A
2012 CANADA	0	0	0		
2013 CANADA	7	0	72		
2014 CANADA	4	1	93		
2015 CANADA	15	11	1003	1g	
2016 CANADA	20	18	1643	3g	3a
2017 CANADA	10	10	900		
2018 CANADA	12	11	990	1g	1a
2019 CANADA	15	14	1305		4a
2020 CANADA	8	6	610	2g	1a
2021 CANADA	10	10	950		2a
2022 CANADA	12	12	1012	1g	3a
2023 CANADA	13	13	1061		4a
FIRST 12 YEARS	126	106	9639	8g	18a

FIFA / OLYMPIC	MP	MS	MIN	G	A
2015 FIFA WC	5	5	436	1g	
2016 OLYMPIC	6	5	495		1a
2019 FIFA WC	4	4	360		1a
2021 OLYMPIC	6	6	590		1a
2023 FIFA WC	3	3	270		

2021 OLYMPIC GAMES • Ashley Lawrence featured in all six matches when Canada won their historic Gold Medal at the Olympic Football Tournament in 2021. She had an assist in the group phase against Great Britain, she scored in the Quarterfinals shootout against Brazil, and she had an important goal-line save in extra time against Sweden in the Final.

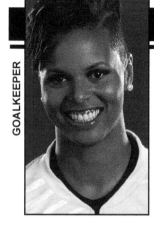

GOALKEEPER

KARINA LeBLANC

Born: 1980-03-30, Atlanta, GA, USA. Grew up in Maple Ridge, BC, CAN. Height 173 cm. Dominant right foot.

5 FIFA World Cups: 1999, 2003, 2007, 2011, 2015
2 Olympic Games: Quarterfinals 2008, Bronze 2012
6 Concacaf: Gold 1998, 2010, Silver 2002, 2008, 2012, Bronze 2004
1st #CANWNT: 1998-07-21 at Montréal, QC, CAN (v. CHN)
1st Clean Sheet: 1999-05-24 at Burnaby, BC, CAN (v. MEX)

CANADA SOCCER HALL OF FAME

Karina LeBlanc won a Bronze Medal from two Olympic Games, featured in five FIFA World Cups, won two Concacaf Championships, and won both a Bronze and Gold Medal from the Pan American Games.

She retired as Canada's all-time leader in appearances by a goalkeeper (110) and clean sheets (47).

She twice helped Canada set program records for unbeaten streaks (2003 and 2010-11). She also led Canada in clean sheets six times and set a Canada record with eight clean sheets in 2010, four of which were recorded at the Concacaf Championship.

At the club level, LeBlanc played football in Canada and the United States. She won a WUSA regular season title in 2003, a WPS regular season title in 2009, and an NWSL Championship playoff title in 2013. She was the USL W-League Goalkeeper of the Year in 2005.

CANADA RECORDS

"A" RECORDS		MP	MS	MIN		CS
1998	CANADA	1	0	45	0	CS
1999	CANADA	3	3	270	1	CS
2000	CANADA	9	9	810	1	CS
2001	CANADA	5	4	405	1	CS
2002	CANADA	8	8	724	5	CS
2003	CANADA	10	10	833	5	CS
2004	CANADA	6	6	519	3	CS
2005	CANADA	7	7	585	2	CS
2006	CANADA	2	2	136	2	CS
2007	CANADA	6	5	495	4	CS
2008	CANADA	8	6	651	4	CS
2009	CANADA	6	6	540	1	CS
2010	CANADA	12	11	1035	8	CS
2011	CANADA	12	11	975	4	CS
2012	CANADA	8	8	720	3	CS
2013	CANADA	4	3	270	2	CS
2014	CANADA	2	2	135	1	CS
2015	CANADA	1	0	45		CS
18 SEASONS		**110**	**101**	**9193**	**47**	**CS**

FIFA / OLYMPIC		MP	MS	MIN	G	A
1999	FIFA WC	0	0	0		
2003	FIFA WC	1	1	90	0	CS
2007	FIFA WC	0	0	0		
2008	OLYMPIC	1	0	101	0	CS
2011	FIFA WC	1	1	90	0	CS
2012	OLYMPIC	1	1	90	1	CS
2015	FIFA WC	0	0	0		

● ● ●

2011 PAN AMERICAN GAMES • Goalkeeper Karina LeBlanc earned Player of the Match honours when Canada captured a Gold Medal at the 2011 Pan American Games in Mexico. Canada won on kicks from the penalty mark after a 1-1 draw with Brazil. In the shootout, LeBlanc saved penalty attempts by Grazielle and Débinha for the 4-3 win.

7

JANET LEMIEUX

Born: 1961-07-29, Edmonton, AB, CAN. Height 160 cm. Dominant right foot.

1st #CANWNT: 1986-07-07 at Blaine, MN, USA (v. USA)

CANADA SOCCER HALL OF FAME

Janet Lemieux was an original member of Canada's National Team in 1986 and she represented her country the following year at the 1987 World Invitational Tournament. In the program's first two years, she played every Canada match until she was ruled out through injury at that 1987 tournament.

Lemieux incidentally featured at midfield in Canada's first international match on 7 July, a 2-0 loss to the Americans at the first North America Cup. She featured at centre back in every match thereafter in 1986 and 1987, starting with Canada's historic 2-1 win over the Americans on 9 July 1986.

Lemieux made six "A" appearances, but played eight matches in total including two tournament matches at the second North America Cup in July 1987. She suffered an irreparable left knee injury later that year, played her last two international matches at the December 1987 tournament, then had career-ending knee surgery in April 1988.

Lemieux played her club football in Canada where she joined the Edmonton Angels for a string of four-straight national titles from 1983 to 1986.

Lemieux did not play soccer in 1982 when the Angels won their first Canadian title and she was ruled out through injury in 1988 when the Angels won their sixth title.

Before joining the Angels in 1983, Lemieux won back-to-back Edmonton First Division titles with Edmonton Ajax SC (1980, 1981).

CANADA RECORDS

"A" RECORDS	MP	MS	MIN	G	A
1986 CANADA	2	2	180		
1987 CANADA	4	4	310		
2 SEASONS	**6**	**6**	**490**		

1986 NORTH AMERICA CUP • Centre back Janet Lemieux made her Canada debut in their first international series against the United States at the 1986 North America Cup. Canada lost the first match 2-0, came back to win the second match 2-1, but then lost the series after the Americans won a 30-minute mini match immediately following the Canada win.

FORWARD / W

19

ADRIANA LEON

Born: 1992-10-02, Mississauga, ON, CAN. Grew up in Maple & King City, ON, CAN. Height 161 cm. Dominant right foot.

3 FIFA World Cups: Canada 2015, France 2019, AU NZ 2023
1 Olympic Games: Gold at Tokyo in 2021
3 Concacaf medals: Silver in 2018, 2020, 2022
1st #CANWNT: 2013-01-12 at Yongchuan, CHN (v. CHN)
1st Goal: 2013-01-12 at Yongchuan, CHN (v. CHN)

OLYMPIC CHAMPION

Adriana Leon has already represented Canada at one FIFA youth tournament, three FIFA World Cups and one Olympic Games. In 2024, she was named to the Best XI at the Concacaf W Gold Cup.

In 2021, she helped Canada set a program record with a 12-match undefeated streak including their first Olympic Gold Medal.

In April 2024, she moved into third place on Canada's all-time goalscoring list. She co-led Canada in goals scored in 2021, 2022 and 2023.

Back in 2013, she scored her first goal in her international debut. In 2018, she scored two goals in the match that qualified Canada to the FIFA World Cup.

ASTON VILLA FC

Leon joined Aston Villa FC ahead of the 2023-24 season. Before the FIFA World Cup, she briefly played with Portland Thorns FC in the NWSL.

Since turning pro, Leon has played her soccer in USA, Switzerland and England. She won the College Cup in 2010 with the University of Notre Dame.

CANADA RECORDS

"A" RECORDS		MP	MS	MIN	G	A
2011	CANADA	0	0	0		
2012	CANADA	0	0	0		
2013	CANADA	16	12	994	3g	
2014	CANADA	9	7	414	1g	
2015	CANADA	13	5	582	1g	
2017	CANADA	6	1	226	3g	
2018	CANADA	10	1	250	6g	2a
2019	CANADA	9	1	236	1g	
2020	CANADA	3	2	155	4g	1a
2021	CANADA	12	4	491	4g	
2022	CANADA	14	9	802	5g	2a
2023	CANADA	13	11	807	3g	1a
FIRST 13 YEARS		**105**	**53**	**4957**	**31g**	**6a**

FIFA / OLYMPIC		MP	MS	MIN	G	A
2015	FIFA WC	4	1	139		
2019	FIFA WC	3	0	54		
2021	OLYMPIC	5	1	188	1g	
2023	FIFA WC	3	3	187	1g	

● ● ●

2021 OLYMPIC GAMES • Adriana Leon made five appearances at the 2021 Olympic Football Tournament when Canada won their Gold Medal in Japan. In Kashima, she scored in Canada's 1-1 draw with Great Britain to clinch a spot in the knockout phase. Three days later in Rishu, she scored in the shootout when Canada eliminated Brazil in the Quarterfinals.

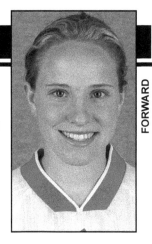

FORWARD

SARA MAGLIO

Born: 1978-03-17, North Vancouver, BC, CAN. Grew up in Coquitlam, BC, CAN. Height 168 cm.

1 FIFA World Cup: Group phase at USA 1999
1st #CANWNT: 1997-06-07 at Oakford, PA, USA (v. AUS)

INTERNATIONAL CAREER

Sara Maglio was just 21 years old when she represented Canada at the FIFA Women's World Cup USA 1999. She was one of just six players aged 22 or younger selected by Head Coach Neil Turnbull.

In 1997, she made her international debut as a teenager in Oakford, Pennsylvania, a 3-2 loss to Australia in extra time.

She got her next chance with Canada in 1999 and won herself a spot on Canada's FIFA World Cup team.

CLUB CAREER

Maglio played her club football in Canada where she won the 2004 USL W-League Championship with Vancouver Whitecaps FC. Maglio made one appearance in the playoffs that season.

Maglio was part of the Vancouver squad when they launched in 2001 known as the Breakers. They reached the USL W-League Final in 2001 before they lost to the Boston Renegades.

Maglio played her college soccer at Simon Fraser University where she won the NAIA Championship in 1996. Across her college career, she was a NAIA All-American four times.

After her time with the Whitecaps, she played for Surrey United SC in the Metro League. She won a runners up medal at Canada Soccer's National Championships in 2007.

CANADA RECORDS

"A" RECORDS	MP	MS	MIN	G	A
1997 CANADA	1	0	45		
1999 CANADA	4	0	83		
2000 CANADA	0	0	0		
3 SEASONS	**5**	**0**	**128**		

FIFA / OLYMPIC	MP	MS	MIN	G	A
1999 FIFA WC	1	0	10		

1999 FIFA WORLD CUP • Sara Maglio made one appearance at the 1999 FIFA Women's World Cup in the United States when Canada were eliminated from the group phase for the second time in a row. She featured as a late substitute in Canada's 4-1 loss to Russia with 29,401 spectators in attendance at Giants Stadium in East Rutherford.

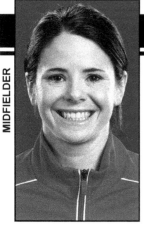

MIDFIELDER

8

DIANA MATHESON

Born: 1984-04-06, Mississauga, ON, CAN. Grew up in Oakville, ON, CAN. Height 153 cm. Dominant right foot.

4 FIFA World Cups: 2003, 2007, 2011, 2015
3 Olympic Games: 2008 Quarterfinals, Bronze in 2012 and 2016
6 Concacaf: Gold 2010, Silver 2006, 2008, 2016, 2018, Bronze 2004
1st #CANWNT: 2003-03-18 at Santo António, POR (v. NOR)
1st Goal: 2003-06-15 at Mazatlán, SI, MEX (v. MEX)

OLYMPIC BRONZE MEDAL

Diana Matheson represented Canada at four FIFA World Cups and three Olympic Games. She retired ranked second with Canada in all-time appearances as well as assists. She set the Canada record with 45 consecutive appearances from 2003 to 2006 (since passed). She was also a three-time runner up in voting for the Player of the Year award.

She won back-to-back Olympic Bronze Medals in 2012 and 2016. She also won the Concacaf Championship in 2010 and the Pan American Games Gold Medal in 2011.

She played in 12 straight FIFA World Cup matches from 2003 to 2011, but missed most of the 2015 FIFA World Cup while recovering from an injury. Through more injuries, she missed the 2019 FIFA World Cup and retired before the 2021 Olympic Games.

Across her club career, Matheson played football in Canada, USA and Norway. She won a league title in Norway in 2012 and reached the NWSL Final in 2016. She was named to the NWSL Best XI in 2013.

CANADA RECORDS

"A" RECORDS	MP	MS	MIN	G	A
2003 CANADA	19	14	1378	1g	1a
2004 CANADA	10	9	764		1a
2005 CANADA	10	10	863		1a
2006 CANADA	16	15	1430		
2007 CANADA	14	13	1187	2g	1a
2008 CANADA	18	18	1634	1g	2a
2009 CANADA	7	7	628		1a
2010 CANADA	15	13	1188	5g	
2011 CANADA	21	21	1876	1g	4a
2012 CANADA	11	11	1009	2g	2a
2013 CANADA	17	17	1515	1g	3a
2014 CANADA	8	8	704	2g	4a
2015 CANADA	5	3	304	1g	1a
2016 CANADA	20	16	1396	1g	1a
2017 CANADA	0	0	0		
2018 CANADA	10	7	641	1g	2a
2019 CANADA	2	1	110		
2020 CANADA	3	0	88	1g	1a
18 SEASONS	**206**	**183**	**16,715**	**19g**	**25g**

FIFA / OLYMPIC	MP	MS	MIN	G	A
2003 FIFA WC	6	6	540		1a
2007 FIFA WC	3	3	264		
2008 OLYMPIC	4	4	364		
2011 FIFA WC	3	3	270		
2012 OLYMPIC	6	6	570	1g	1a
2015 FIFA WC	1	0	28		
2016 OLYMPIC	6	4	322		

● ● ●

2012 OLYMPIC GAMES • Diana Matheson heroically scored the 1-0 match winner when Canada won their inspiring Bronze Medal at the London 2012 Olympic Football Tournament. Across six matches, she was one of three Canadians who featured in every minute of the tournament including their final match against France.

JOAN McEACHERN

MIDFIELDER

Born: 1963-04-12, Leroy, SK, CAN. Height 170 cm. Dominant right foot.

1 FIFA International Tournament: Quarterfinals at China 1988
1 FIFA World Cup: Group phase at Sweden 1995
3 Concacaf medals: Silver 1991 and 1994, Bronze 1993
1st #CANWNT: 1987-07-05 at Blaine, MN, USA (v. SWE)
1st Goal: 1988-06-03 at Foshan, CHN (v. CIV)

CANADA SOCCER HALL OF FAME

Joan McEachern represented Canada at their first FIFA World Cup in 1995 after she played at both the 1987 World Invitational Tournament and FIFA's 1988 International Football Tournament.

In 1991, she helped Canada finish second at the inaugural Concacaf Championship in Haiti, but only the winners USA qualified for the FIFA World Cup that year.

Three years later, she finished second at the 1994 Concacaf Championship, but this time Canada qualified for their first FIFA World Cup.

From 1987 to 1995, McEachern made 31 career international "A" appearances, which at the time ranked sixth all time for Canada. She was 24 years old when she made her international debut on 5 July 1987 at the second North America Cup.

At the club level, McEachern played her club football in Canada where she won the Jubilee Trophy four times at the National Championships. She won the title three times with the Edmonton Angels (1985, 1986, 1988) and once with Coquitlam Metro-Ford SC (1994).

She was the National Championships' Most Valuable Player in 1985 and she scored the series winner in both 1985 and 1994.

CANADA RECORDS

"A" RECORDS	MP	MS	MIN	G	A
1987 CANADA	7	6	xx		
1988 CANADA	4	4	320	1g	
1989 CANADA	0	0	0		
1990 CANADA	5	5	342		2a
1991 CANADA	5	5	375	1g	
1993 CANADA	3	3	201		
1994 CANADA	2	0	25		
1995 CANADA	5	5	350		
8 SEASONS	**31**	**28**	**n/a**	**2g**	**2a**

FIFA / OLYMPIC	MP	MS	MIN	G	A
1988 FIFA	4	4	320	1g	
1995 FIFA WC	0	0	0		

1988 FIFA INTERNATIONAL TOURNAMENT • Joan McEachern played in every Canada minute at FIFA's first women's international tournament in June 1988. She scored her first international goal in the 6-0 win over Côte d'Ivoire in the group phase. Five days later, Canada were eliminated in the Quarterfinals after a narrow 1-0 loss to Sweden.

GOALKEEPER

1

ERIN McLEOD

Born: 1995-01-06, St. Albert, AB, CAN. Grew up in Edmonton & Calgary, AB, CAN. Height 174 cm. Dominant right foot.

4 FIFA World Cups: 2003, 2007, 2011, 2015
3 Olympic Games: 2008, Bronze 2012, Gold 2021
6 Concacaf: Silver 2002, 2006, 2008, 2012, 2016, Bronze 2004
1st #CANWNT: 2002-03-30 at Lagoa, POR (v. WAL)
1st Clean Sheet: 2002-03-30 at Lagoa, POR (v. WAL)

OLYMPIC CHAMPION

Erin McLeod won a FIFA Silver Medal at the first FIFA U-19 World Championship, played in four FIFA World Cups, and won two medals from three Olympic Games. She left international football as Canada's all-time leader in appearances by a goalkeeper.

She won an Olympic Bronze Medal in 2012 and an Olympic Gold Medal in 2021.

Across her four FIFA World Cups, McLeod started 11 straight Canada matches from 2007 to 2015. At their home FIFA World Cup in 2015, she helped Canada reach the Quarterfinals.

STJARNAN FC

McLeod joined Stjarnan FC in Iceland ahead of the 2023 season. Across her career, she has also played club football in Canada, USA, Sweden and Germany, including UEFA Champions League with FC Rosengård. Early in her career, she was a two-time USL W-League Championship winner with Vancouver Whitecaps FC.

CANADA RECORDS

"A" RECORDS		MP	MS	MIN		CS
2002	CANADA	6	6	540	2	CS
2003	CANADA	6	5	465	0	CS
2004	CANADA	2	1	111	0	CS
2006	CANADA	14	14	1277	3	CS
2007	CANADA	6	6	529	2	CS
2008	CANADA	18	18	1534	6	CS
2009	CANADA	1	1	90	0	CS
2010	CANADA	3	3	225	1	CS
2011	CANADA	11	10	899	5	CS
2012	CANADA	13	13	1200	6	CS
2013	CANADA	13	13	1080	8	CS
2014	CANADA	7	6	585	1	CS
2015	CANADA	12	12	1025	7	CS
2016	CANADA	3	3	270	2	CS
2017	CANADA	0	0	0		
2018	CANADA	1	1	90	1	CS
2019	CANADA	2	2	135	1	CS
2021	CANADA	1	0	43	1	CS
2022	CANADA	0	0	0		
19 SEASONS		119	114	10,098	46	CS

FIFA / OLYMPIC		MP	MS	MIN		CS
2003	FIFA WC	0	0	0		
2007	FIFA WC	3	3	259	1	CS
2008	OLYMPIC	4	4	289	0	CS
2011	FIFA WC	3	3	270	0	CS
2012	OLYMPIC	5	5	480	2	CS
2015	FIFA WC	5	5	450	3	CS
2021	OLYMPIC	0	0	0		

● ● ●

2012 OLYMPIC GAMES • Erin McLeod featured in five of Canada's six matches at the London 2012 Olympic Football Tournament when they won their inspiring Bronze Medal. She was at her best in Canada's last match when she earned Player of the Match honours and posted a clean sheet for the 1-0 victory over France.

16

LUCE MONGRAIN

CENTRE BACK / RB

Born: 1971-01-11, Trois-Rivières, QC, CAN. Height 173 cm. Dominant right foot.

1 FIFA World Cup: Group phase at Sweden 1995
3 Concacaf medals: Silver 1991 and 1994, Bronze 1993
1st #CANWNT: 1987-12-11 at Kaohsiung City, TPE (v. HKG)

CANADA SOCCER HALL OF FAME

Luce Mongrain represented Canada at their first FIFA World Cup in 1995. It marked the pinnacle of her nine-year international career that started with the 1987 World Invitational Tournament. When she left the international game, she ranked seventh all time with 30 international "A" appearances.

When she made her debut in December 1987, she was still just 16 years old, the program's youngest debutant until Christine Sinclair came along in March 2000.

Mongrain helped Canada finish in second place at the 1991 Concacaf Championship, but at the time only the champions USA advanced to the FIFA World Cup. When they finished in second place at the Concacaf Championship in 1994, both the champions USA and runners up Canada qualified for the 1995 FIFA World Cup.

In club football, Mongrain played in both Canada and the United States. She played for both Dorval United SC and Lakeshore SC in Québec.

She initially played her college soccer in the United States at North Carolina State University, then moved back to Canada where she played at McGill University. In 1991, she helped McGill reach the CIAU Final. She was also named a Second Team All-Canadian.

CANADA RECORDS

"A" RECORDS	MP	MS	MIN	G	A
1987 CANADA	4	4	280		
1989 CANADA	0	0	0		
1990 CANADA	2	1	110		
1991 CANADA	3	2	182		
1993 CANADA	5	5	450		
1994 CANADA	10	8	730		
1995 CANADA	6	4	378		
7 SEASONS	30	24	2130		

FIFA / OLYMPIC	MP	MS	MIN	G	A
1995 FIFA WC	1	1	90		

1995 FIFA WORLD CUP • Luce Mongrain made one appearance at Canada's first FIFA Women's World Cup at Sweden 1995. She played the full 90 minutes of Canada's second group match, a 3-3 draw with Nigeria on 8 June in Helsingborg. It was her last international appearance with Canada.

LEFT BACK

ISABELLE MORNEAU

Born: 1976-04-18, Greenfield, QC, CAN. Grew up in Longueuil, QC, CAN. Height 163 cm. Dominant left foot.

3 FIFA World Cups: Group phase 1995, 1999, 4th Place 2003
3 Concacaf medals: 1998 Gold, 2006 Silver, 2004 Bronze
1st #CANWNT: 1995-04-11 at Poissy, FRA (v. FRA)
1st Goal: 1997-06-04 at Worcester, MA, USA (v. ITA)

CANADA SOCCER HALL OF FAME

Isabelle Morneau represented Canada at three FIFA World Cups from 1995 to 2003 and she was part of their first Concacaf Championship in women's football in 1998. When she left international football in 2006, she ranked fourth all time with 87 career appearances for Canada.

In 1998, Morneau started all five matches at the Concacaf Championship as Canada went undefeated with no goals conceded at Toronto's Centennial Stadium. They beat Mexico 1-0 in the Final.

In 2003, she helped Canada set a program record with a 10-match undefeated streak before the FIFA World Cup. She also helped Canada earn their best result at a FIFA World Cup when they finished in fourth place at USA 2003.

She was just 18 years old when she made her 1995 international debut in a 1-0 loss to France. Eleven years later, she made her last appearance when they captured Silver at the 2006 Concacaf Gold Cup.

Morneau played her club football in Canada and the United States. Growing up, she played her youth soccer in Québec. She played her college soccer at the University of Nebraska where she was a two-time NSCAA Second-Team All-American.

CANADA RECORDS

"A" RECORDS	MP	MS	MIN	G	A
1995 CANADA	3	1	135		
1996 CANADA	5	5	337		
1997 CANADA	3	3	280	1g	1a
1998 CANADA	8	8	683	3g	
1999 CANADA	7	7	585		
2000 CANADA	14	13	1149		1a
2001 CANADA	3	3	270		
2002 CANADA	10	10	872	2g	
2003 CANADA	8	2	201		1a
2004 CANADA	8	2	353		
2005 CANADA	9	7	595		
2006 CANADA	9	5	417		
12 SEASONS	**87**	**66**	**5877**	**6g**	**3a**

FIFA / OLYMPIC	MP	MS	MIN	G	A
1995 FIFA WC	0	0	0		
1999 FIFA WC	3	3	270		
2003 FIFA WC	3	2	108		

● ● ●

FIFA WORLD CUPS • Isabelle Morneau made six appearances across three FIFA World Cups from Sweden 1995 to USA 2003, including Canada's fourth-place finish in 2003. Canada's only teenager in 1995, she made her FIFA World Cup debut four years later when she featured in every Canada minute at USA 1999.

CARMELINA MOSCATO

CENTRE BACK / M

Born: 1984-05-21, Mississauga, ON, CAN. Height 171 cm. Dominant right foot.

3 FIFA World Cups: 2003, 2011 and 2015
1 Olympic Games: Bronze at 2012
4 Concacaf medals: Gold 2010, Silver 2002, 2012, Bronze 2004
1st #CANWNT: 2002-04-03 at Poitiers, FRA (v. AUS)
1st Goal: 2003-03-20 at Guia, POR (v. GRE)

CANADA SOCCER HALL OF FAME

Carmelina Moscato won an Olympic Bronze Medal, represented Canada at three FIFA World Cups, and won a Concacaf Championship as an international footballer. She made 94 international "A" appearances across 14 years with Canada.

She won a FIFA Silver Medal at the first FIFA U-19 World Championship in 2002 and was named a tournament all-star.

She twice helped Canada set program records for unbeaten streaks (2003 and 2010-11). She made her FIFA World Cup debut against the Americans in Canada's last match at USA 2003 when they finished in fourth place.

She was just 17 years old when she made her Canada debut one year earlier in a 0-0 draw with Australia.

At the club level, she played her football in Canada, USA, Italy and Sweden. She won the USL W-League Championship with Vancouver Whitecaps FC in 2004, then

reached the Final with Ottawa Fury FC in 2005 and 2006. She helped Seattle Reign FC reach the NWSL Final in 2014.

CANADA RECORDS

"A" RECORDS	MP	MS	MIN	G	A
2002 CANADA	8	5	419		1a
2003 CANADA	7	1	164	1g	
2004 CANADA	6	2	277	1g	
2006 CANADA	1	0	45		
2009 CANADA	3	1	90		
2010 CANADA	17	14	1254		
2011 CANADA	13	9	696		
2012 CANADA	15	13	1274		
2013 CANADA	12	11	854		
2014 CANADA	3	2	169		
2015 CANADA	9	6	503		
11 SEASONS	**94**	**64**	**5745**	**2g**	**1a**

FIFA / OLYMPIC	MP	MS	MIN	G	A
2003 FIFA WC	1	0	1		
2011 FIFA WC	0	0	0		
2012 LONDON	6	6	570		
2015 FIFA WC	2	1	112		

2012 OLYMPIC GAMES • Centre back Carmelina Moscato featured in every Canada minute when Canada won their Bronze Medal at the Olympic Football Tournament in 2012. She helped Canada post clean sheets against South Africa in the group phase, against Great Britain in the Quarterfinals, and against France in the Bronze Medal match.

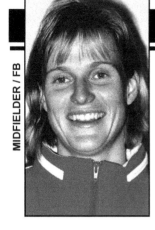

MIDFIELDER / FB

SUZANNE MUIR

Born: 1970-07-06, Brockville, ON, CAN. Grew up in Dartmouth, NS, CAN. Height 173 cm. Dominant right foot.

2 FIFA World Cups: Group phase in 1995 and 1999
1 Concacaf medal: Gold in 1998
1st #CANWNT: 1995-04-11 at Poissy, FRA (v. FRA)
1st Goal: 1998-08-28 FWCQ at Toronto, ON, CAN (v. PUR)

CANADA SOCCER HALL OF FAME

Suzanne Muir represented Canada at two FIFA World Cups and she was part of their first Concacaf Championship in women's football. She made 31 career international appearances which in 1999 ranked tied for ninth in program history.

In 1998, Muir played every minute at the Concacaf Championship as Canada went undefeated without conceding a goal. In the Final at Toronto's Centennial Stadium, Muir initiated the play for the only goal of the match: her throw-in from the right side to Shannon Rosenow was relayed into a cross from which Liz Smith headed in the 1-0 match winner.

Muir made her international debut in 1995 at right back in a 1-0 loss to France. She played in a career-high nine matches that year including Canada's first participation at the FIFA World Cup.

At the club level, Muir played her football in Canada where she won one national title and earned five runners-up medals. After finishing second three years in a row with Dartmouth City Mazda (1990 to 1992), she won the Jubilee Trophy with Coquitlam Metro-Ford SC in 1994. She again reached the Final in 1998 with Vancouver UBC Alumni and 2001 with Sackville's Scotia Olympics.

Across her career, she won five provincial titles in Nova Scotia and three provincial titles in British Columbia. In 1993, she won a Canada Games Silver Medal with Nova Scotia.

CANADA RECORDS

"A" RECORDS		MP	MS	MIN	G	A
1994	CANADA	0	0	0		
1995	CANADA	9	7	651		
1996	CANADA	5	5	450		
1997	CANADA	3	3	280		
1998	CANADA	8	8	648	2g	1a
1999	CANADA	6	3	318		
6 SEASONS		31	26	2347	2g	1a

FIFA / OLYMPIC		MP	MS	MIN	G	A
1995	FIFA WC	2	1	97		
1999	FIFA WC	0	0	0		

● ● ●

FIFA WORLD CUPS • Suzanne Muir was one of just seven players that represented Canada across their first two FIFA World Cups in 1995 and 1999. She made her FIFA World Cup debut as a substitute in the 3-2 loss to England, then got her first start four days later in the group finale against Norway.

LEFT BACK

MARIE-EVE NAULT

Born: 1982-02-16, Trois-Rivières, QC, CAN. Height 169 cm. Dominant left foot.

2 FIFA World Cups: Group phase in 2011, Quarterfinals in 2015
1 Olympic Games: Bronze at London 2012
2 Concacaf medals: Gold in 2010, Bronze in 2004
1st #CANWNT: 2004-01-30 at Shenzhen, CHN (v. CHN)

OLYMPIC BRONZE MEDAL

Marie-Eve Nault represented Canada at two FIFA World Cups and one Olympic Games. She won a Bronze Medal in 2012 and she was an alternate when Canada reached the podium for the second time in 2016.

From late 2010 to early 2011, she helped Canada set a program record with an 11-match undefeated streak. Inside that streak, she helped Canada win the 2010 Concacaf Championship.

From 2003 to 2017, Nault made 71 career international appearances. After her first call up in December 2003, she made her debut in a 2-1 loss to China on 30 January 2004 in Shenzhen.

In February 2017, Nault was honoured with the captain's armband for her last Canada match before her retirement.

CLUB CAREER

Nault played her club football in Canada, USA and Sweden. She reached the USL W-League Final with Ottawa Fury FC in

2006. In Sweden, she helped KIF Örebro finish second in the 2014 Damallsvenskan league standings and then reach the Round of 16 in 2015-16 UEFA Champions League.

She was honoured by the Soccer Québec Hall of Fame in 2022.

CANADA RECORDS

"A" RECORDS	MP	MS	MIN	G	A
2003 CANADA	0	0	0		
2004 CANADA	8	7	569		2a
2009 CANADA	6	1	207		
2010 CANADA	17	14	1294		
2011 CANADA	14	11	925		
2012 CANADA	8	4	431		
2013 CANADA	5	3	300		
2014 CANADA	7	6	360		
2015 CANADA	5	2	189		
2016 CANADA	0	0	0		
2017 CANADA	1	1	90		
11 SEASONS	**71**	**49**	**4365**		**2a**

FIFA / OLYMPIC	MP	MS	MIN	G	A
2011 FIFA WC	2	2	135		
2012 OLYMPIC	4	4	360		
2015 FIFA WC	1	0	2		
2016 OLYMPIC	-	-	-		

2012 OLYMPIC GAMES • Marie-Eve Nault made four appearances at the London 2012 Olympic Football Tournament when Canada won their inspiring Bronze Medal. In the unforgettable Semifinals at Old Trafford, Nault was part of the build up that led to Christine Sinclair's first of three goals against the Americans.

MIDFIELDER / FB

5

ANDREA NEIL

Born: 1971-10-26, Vancouver, BC, CAN.   Height 177 cm. Dominant left foot.

4 FIFA World Cups: 1995, 1999, 2003, 2007
5 Concacaf medals: Silver 1991, 1994, 2002, 2006, Bronze 2004
1st #CANWNT: 1991-04-19 FWCQ at Port-au-Prince, HAI (v. JAM)
1st Goal: 1994-08-13 FWCQ at Montréal, QC, CAN (v. JAM)

CANADA SOCCER HALL OF FAME

Andrea Neil was the first Canadian to play at four FIFA World Cups from 1995 to 2007. She won five Concacaf medals plus Bronze at the 2007 Pan American Games in Rio. She retired as Canada's all-time leader with 132 international "A" appearances.

Neil was Canada Soccer's Player of the Year in 2001. Two years later, she helped Canada set a program record with a 10-match undefeated streak.

Neil was just 19 years old when she made her debut in Port-au-Prince, Haiti at the 1991 Concacaf Championship. She made her last appearances in Hangzhou, China at the 2007 FIFA World Cup.

Neil played her club football in Canada where she helped Vancouver Whitecaps FC win the USL W-League Championship in 2004 and 2006. She previously reached the Final in 2001. Earlier in her career, she helped Coquitlam Metro-Ford SC lift the Jubilee Trophy at Canada Soccer's 1994 National Championships.

At the University of British Columbia, Neil won the 1993 CIAU Championship. She was a First Team All-Canadian in 1994.

CANADA RECORDS

"A" RECORDS	MP	MS	MIN	G	A
1990 CANADA	0	0	0		
1991 CANADA	1	0	25		
1993 CANADA	2	1	135		
1994 CANADA	8	8	654	2g	
1995 CANADA	8	6	563		
1996 CANADA	5	5	422		
1997 CANADA	2	2	180		
1999 CANADA	3	0	154	1g	1a
2000 CANADA	16	12	xx	3g	1a
2001 CANADA	11	8	709		
2002 CANADA	13	13	1082	5g	1a
2003 CANADA	20	20	1695	7g	1a
2004 CANADA	9	9	612	1g	1a
2005 CANADA	7	4	345	2g	1a
2006 CANADA	16	5	541	1g	1a
2007 CANADA	11	5	378	2g	
16 SEASONS	132	98	7495	24g	7a

FIFA / OLYMPIC	MP	MS	MIN	G	A
1995 FIFA WC	3	2	185		
1999 FIFA WC	2	0	109		1a
2003 FIFA WC	5	5	436		
2007 FIFA WC	1	0	6		

● ● ●

1995 FIFA WORLD CUP • Andrea Neil featured in all three Canada matches when they made their debut at the FIFA Women's World Cup in 1995. Neil lined up along the backline at left back for Canada's first two matches against England and Nigeria. She then featured as a late substitute in Canada's group finale against the 1995 world champions Norway.

CENTRE BACK

SHAROLTA NONEN

Born: 1977-12-30, Vancouver, BC, CAN. Height 168 cm. Dominant right foot.

2 FIFA World Cups: Group phase 1999, 4th Place 2003
2 Concacaf medals Silver in 2002, Bronze in 2004
1st #CANWNT: 1999-06-03 at Portland, OR, USA (v. BRA)
1st Goal: 2003-03-16 at Ferreiras, POR (v. SWE)

INTERNATIONAL CAREER

Sharolta Nonen represented Canada at two FIFA World Cups including a fourth-place finish at USA 2003. She helped Canada set a program record with a 10-match undefeated streak in 2003.

At the 2002 Concacaf Gold Cup, Nonen set up the match winner that qualified Canada to the 2003 FIFA World Cup. Her long free kick was headed backwards by Dioselina Valderrama into Mexico's own goal.

Across eight years from 1999 to 2006, she made 63 career appearances which at the time ranked ninth most in program history. She was 21 years old when she made her international "A" debut on 3 June 1999 (just 16 days before the FIFA World Cup).

CLUB CAREER

Nonen played her club football in Canada, USA and Denmark. In the inaugural 2001 WUSA season, she helped the Atlanta Beat finish first overall in the regular season, then finish as runners up in the playoffs. She also helped Atlanta reach the WUSA Final

in 2003 and then the Los Angeles Sol reach the WPS Final in 2009.

In 2007, she helped the Atlanta Silverbacks finish as runners up in the USL W-League playoffs.

Nonen played her college soccer at the University of Nebraska. As a youth player, she helped British Columbia win the 1997 Canada Games Tournament.

CANADA RECORDS

"A" RECORDS	MP	MS	MIN	G	A
1999 CANADA	7	7	630		1a
2000 CANADA	8	8	720		1a
2001 CANADA	11	11	928		
2002 CANADA	11	11	975		
2003 CANADA	14	14	1254	1g	
2004 CANADA	7	7	630		
2006 CANADA	5	5	450		
7 SEASONS	63	63	5587	1g	2a

FIFA / OLYMPIC	MP	MS	MIN	G	A
1999 FIFA WC	3	3	270		
2003 FIFA WC	6	6	540		

FIFA WORLD CUPS • Sharolta Nonen featured in every Canada minute across back-to-back FIFA World Cups in the United States. She made three appearances in 1999 when Canada were eliminated in the group phase, then made six more appearances in 2003 when Canada finished in fourth place.

MIDFIELDER / FB

VERONICA O'BRIEN

Born: 1971-01-29, Barrie, ON, CAN. Grew up in Orangeville, ON, CAN. Height 178 cm. Dominant right foot.

1 FIFA World Cup: Group phase at Sweden 1995
2 Concacaf medals: Silver in 1994, Bronze in 1993
1st #CANWNT: 1990-07-23 at Winnipeg, MB, CAN (v. NOR)
1st Goal: 1994-07-25 at Ottawa, ON, CAN (v. CHN)

INTERNATIONAL CAREER

Veronica O'Brien represented Canada at their first FIFA Women's World Cup in 1995. She won Concacaf medals in both 1993 and 1994.

She made her international "A" debut in Canada's first-ever home international match, a 2-0 loss to Norway at the Winnipeg Soccer Complex on 23 July 1990.

In 1993, O'Brien represented Canada at the World University Games in July and then captured Bronze at the Concacaf Invitational Tournament in August. The next year, she helped Canada qualify for the FIFA World Cup and capture a Silver Medal at the 1994 Concacaf Championship in Montréal.

From 1990 to 1997, O'Brien played in 31 career international "A" matches and scored one goal (25 July 1994 against China).

CLUB CAREER

O'Brien played her club football in Canada and her college soccer in the United States.

She played four seasons at the University of New Hampshire and was a three-time All-North Atlantic Conference selection.

At the youth level, she represented Ontario at the 1993 Canada Games. She played her club football with the Oakville Angels.

She was honoured by the University of New Hampshire Athletics Hall of Fame in 2002.

CANADA RECORDS

"A" RECORDS	MP	MS	MIN	G	A
1990 CANADA	1	1	xx		
1991 CANADA	0	0	0		
1993 CANADA	6	5	475		
1994 CANADA	10	10	820	1g	
1995 CANADA	7	6	502		
1996 CANADA	5	5	450		
1997 CANADA	2	0	45		
7 SEASONS	31	27	2292	1g	

FIFA / OLYMPIC	MP	MS	MIN	G	A
1995 FIFA WC	2	2	151		

● ● ●

1995 FIFA WORLD CUP • Veronica O'Brien made two appearances at Canada's first FIFA Women's World Cup in 1995. She played the full 90 minutes in Canada's first match against England, a 3-2 loss at Helsingborg. She also played two days later when Canada drew 3-3 with Nigeria for their first-ever point at a FIFA World Cup.

15

MIDFIELDER

KELLY PARKER

Born: 1981-03-08, Regina, SK, CAN. Grew up in Saskatoon, SK, CAN. Height 161 cm. Dominant right foot.

1 FIFA World Cup: Group phase at Germany 2011
1 Olympic Games: Bronze at London 2012
1 Concacaf medal: Silver in 2012
1st #CANWNT: 2003-07-17 at Montréal, QC, CAN (v. BRA)
1st Goal: 2010-02-20 at Larnaka, CYP (v. POL)

OLYMPIC BRONZE MEDAL

Kelly Parker represented Canada at one FIFA World Cup and one Olympic Games. She missed Canada's run to the Concacaf Championship in 2010 through injury, but made it back in the squad before the FIFA World Cup in 2011.

She scored her first international goal in February 2010 against Poland. In 2011, she got a key assist on the 1-1 equaliser against USA; in 2012, she got a key assist on the match winner against Mexico that qualified Canada to the Olympic Games.

At London 2012, she featured in three of Canada's six matches as a substitute. She featured in her last international match in the Quarterfinals against Great Britain.

CLUB CAREER

Parker played her club football in Canada, USA and Germany. In Canada, she helped Ottawa Fury FC reach the USL W-League Final in 2005 and 2006. She won the league scoring title in 2003 and was named the Most Valuable Player in 2004. She then

helped Sky Blue FC win the 2009 WPS Championship.

After a stint in Germany and return to the WPS, Parker joined the Buffalo Flash where she won the 2010 USL W-League Championship. She also won her second MVP award.

After her career, she was honoured by the University of Texas El Paso Hall of Fame as well as the Saskatchewan Sports Hall of Fame.

CANADA RECORDS

"A" RECORDS	MP	MS	MIN	G	A
2001 CANADA	0	0	0		
2003 CANADA	1	0	1		
2005 CANADA	0	0	0		
2009 CANADA	5	5	406		
2010 CANADA	6	6	492	1g	1a
2011 CANADA	11	8	884		4a
2012 CANADA	17	11	938	2g	2a
7 SEASONS	40	30	2721	3g	7a

FIFA / OLYMPIC	MP	MS	MIN	G	A
2011 FIFA WC	1	0	45		
2012 OLYMPIC	3	0	28		

2011 PAN AMERICAN GAMES • Midfielder Kelly Parker featured in every Canada minute across five matches when they won a Gold Medal at the 2011 Pan American Games in Mexico. In their opening match of the group phase, she got two assists in a come-from-behind 3-1 victory over Costa Rica.

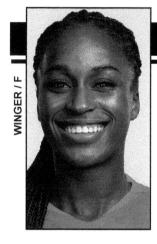

WINGER / F

NICHELLE PRINCE

Born: 1995-02-19, Ajax, ON, CAN. Height 164 cm. Dominant right foot.

2 FIFA World Cups: France 2019, AU NZ 2023
2 Olympic Games: Bronze at Rio 2016, Gold at Tokyo in 2021
4 Concacaf medals: Silver 2016, 2018, 2020, 2022
1st #CANWNT: 2013-01-12 at Yongchuan, CHN (v. CHN)
1st Goal: 2013-01-14 at Yongchuan, CHN (v. KOR)

OLYMPIC CHAMPION

Nichelle Prince has already represented Canada at two FIFA youth tournaments, two FIFA World Cups and two Olympic Games. She helped Canada set a program record with a 12-match undefeated streak in 2021.

She won an Olympic Bronze Medal in 2016 and an Olympic Gold Medal in 2021.

In 2018, Prince led Canada with four assists. In 2019, she scored her first FIFA World Cup goal in a win over New Zealand. She also got an assist in that same match as Canada qualified for the knockout phase for the second tournament in a row.

She was limited to just eight minutes at the 2023 FIFA World Cup after returning from an injury. In September, she helped Canada qualify for the Paris 2024 Olympic Games.

KANSAS CITY CURRENT

Prince joined the Kansas City Current ahead of the 2024 NWSL season. Since turning pro in 2017, she had played seven seasons with the Houston Dash. In 2020, she helped Houston win the NWSL Challenge Cup and finish second in the NWSL Fall Series standings.

Before turning pro, she played her college soccer at Ohio State University.

CANADA RECORDS

"A" RECORDS	MP	MS	MIN	G	A
2012 CANADA	0	0	0		
2013 CANADA	3	0	25	1g	
2015 CANADA	4	2	215	2g	
2016 CANADA	14	2	372	3g	2a
2017 CANADA	11	3	386		2a
2018 CANADA	11	8	614	4g	4a
2019 CANADA	12	10	788	1g	1a
2020 CANADA	4	1	200		1a
2021 CANADA	16	13	875	2g	1a
2022 CANADA	15	10	753	13g	1a
2023 CANADA	6	5	291	3g	1a
FIRST 10 YEARS	96	54	4519	16g	13a

FIFA / OLYMPIC	MP	MS	MIN	G	A
2016 OLYMPIC	3	0	46		
2019 FIFA WC	3	3	223	1g	1a
2021 OLYMPIC	6	5	367		1a
2023 FIFA WC	1	0	8		

● ● ●

2021 OLYMPIC GAMES • Nichelle Prince featured in all six Canada matches when they won their historic Gold Medal at the 2021 Olympic Football Tournament in Japan. In Canada's 2-1 win over Chile in the group phase, she was part of the build up on Janine Beckie's opening goal in the first half and then got an assist on Beckie's second goal early in the second half.

5

MIDFIELDER / CB

QUINN

Born: 1995-08-11, Toronto, ON, CAN. Height 175 cm. Dominant right foot.

2 FIFA World Cups: France 2019, AU NZ 2023
2 Olympic Games: Bronze at Rio 2016, Gold at Tokyo in 2021
4 Concacaf medals: Silver in 2016, 2018, 2020, 2022
1st #CANWNT: 2014-03-07 at Larnaka, CYP (v. ITA)
1st Goal: 2016-02-16 OQ at Houston, TX, USA (v. GUA)

OLYMPIC CHAMPION

Quinn has already represented Canada at two FIFA youth tournaments, two FIFA World Cups and two Olympic Games. In 2021, they helped Canada set a program record with a 12-match undefeated streak as well as win an Olympic Gold Medal at Tokyo.

At Rio 2016, Quinn played in four Canada matches and got two starts. They played the full 90 minutes at centre back in wins over Zimbabwe and Germany. They also got an assist on Melissa Tancredi's match winner against Germany.

In 2018, they were named to the Best XI at the Concacaf Championship.

At both the FIFA World Cup in 2019 and the Olympic Games in 2021, Quinn featured as a midfielder.

SEATTLE REIGN FC

Quinn helped OL Reign FC win the 2022 NWSL Shield as the top team during the regular season. In 2023, they finished fourth in the regular season, but reached the NWSL Final in the playoffs.

Since turning pro in 2018, they have played their club soccer in the United States, France and Sweden. Before turning pro, they played at Duke University.

CANADA RECORDS

"A" RECORDS		MP	MS	MIN	G	A
2014	CANADA	5	2	244		
2015	CANADA	7	3	325		
2016	CANADA	13	5	612	3g	1a
2017	CANADA	8	5	460		1a
2018	CANADA	11	10	902	2g	1a
2019	CANADA	10	4	361		
2020	CANADA	5	3	288		
2021	CANADA	14	12	831		1a
2022	CANADA	8	7	893		
2023	CANADA	15	10	603	1g	
FIRST 9 YEARS		96	61	5519	6g	4a

FIFA / OLYMPIC		MP	MS	MIN	G	A
2016	OLYMPIC	4	2	256		1a
2019	FIFA WC	3	0	24		
2021	OLYMPIC	6	5	336		
2023	FIFA WC	3	3	257		

2021 OLYMPIC GAMES • Quinn featured in all six Canada matches when they won a Gold Medal at the Olympic Football Tournament in Japan. They started five of the six matches, including all three knockout matches when Canada beat Brazil in the Quarterfinals, USA in the Semifinals, and Sweden in the Final.

CENTRE BACK / M

MICHELLE RING

Born: 1967-11-28, Calgary, AB, CAN. Grew up in Mount Lehman, BC, CAN. Height 168 cm. Dominant left foot.

1 FIFA International Tournament: Quarterfinals at China 1988
1 FIFA World Cup: Group phase at Sweden 1995
2 Concacaf medals: Silver in 1994, Bronze in 1993
1st #CANWNT: 1986-07-07 at Blaine, MN, USA (v. USA)
1st Goal: 1994-08-19 FWCQ at Montréal, QC, CAN (v. TRI)

CANADA SOCCER HALL OF FAME

Michelle Ring represented Canada at their first FIFA World Cup in 1995 after featuring at both the World Invitational Tournament in 1987 and FIFA's International Football Tournament in 1988.

One of Canada's original Women's National Team players from 1986, she played every minute of Canada's four matches at the 1988 FIFA tournament, including Canada's narrow 1-0 loss to Sweden in the Quarter-finals.

She then played every minute of the 1993 and 1994 Concacaf tournaments as well as the 1995 FIFA World Cup in Sweden.

From 1986 to 1995, Ring made 45 career international "A" appearances, at the time ranked second all time for Canada.

Ring played her club football in Canada where she helped Surrey Marlins SC win three successive National Championships for the Jubilee Trophy. She earned MVP honours at the 1993 tournament.

With the University of British Columbia, she scored the match winner that captured the CIAU Championship in 1987. Three years later, she helped UBC finish as runners up at another CIAU national tournament.

CANADA RECORDS

"A" RECORDS		MP	MS	MIN	G	A
1986	CANADA	1	1	9		
1987	CANADA	6	5	xx		
1988	CANADA	4	4	320		
1990	CANADA	5	4	xx		1a
1991	CANADA	0	0	0		
1993	CANADA	6	5	495		
1994	CANADA	11	11	990	1g	
1995	CANADA	12	12	970	1g	
8 SEASONS		45	42	n/a	2g	1a

FIFA / OLYMPIC		MP	MS	MIN	G	A
1988	FIFA	4	4	320		
1995	FIFA WC	3	3	270		

● ● ●

1995 FIFA WORLD CUP • Michelle Ring played in every Canada minute at the 1995 FIFA Women's World Cup in Sweden, with all three matches played in a short five-day window in Helsingborg and Gävle. She was one of six original Women's National Team players from 1986 that also represented Canada at their first FIFA World Cup in 1995.

8

RIGHT BACK

JAYDE RIVIERE

Born: 2001-01-22, Markham, ON, CAN. Height 164 cm.
Dominant right foot.

2 FIFA World Cup: France 2019, AU NZ 2023
1 Olympic Games: Gold at Tokyo in 2021
2 Concacaf medals: Silver in 2020 and 2022
1st #CANWNT: 2017-11-12 at San Jose, CA, USA (v. USA)
1st Goal: 2020-01-29 OQ at Edinburg, TX, USA (v. SKN)

OLYMPIC CHAMPION

Jayde Riviere has already represented Canada at two FIFA youth tournaments, two FIFA World Cups and one Olympic Games. In 2021, she helped Canada set a program record with a 12-match undefeated streak including the Olympic Gold Medal in Tokyo.

As a teenager in 2019, she made her FIFA World Cup debut in Canada's second group match at Grenoble against New Zealand. She helped Canada reach the Round of 16 and featured in matches against the Netherlands and Sweden.

In 2020, she scored her first international goal against St. Kitts and Nevis at the Concacaf Olympic Qualifiers in Texas. Incidentally, she scored her first goal in the same match that Christine Sinclair broke the world's all-time international goals record.

MANCHESTER UNITED FC

Riviere turned pro with Manchester United FC during the 2022-23 FA Women's Super League season, but she missed most of the campaign through injury. She made her pro debut on 7 May 2023. In 2023-24, she made two appearances in Qualifying for UEFA Champions League.

Before turning pro, Riviere played her college soccer at the University of Michigan. She previously played in Canada Soccer's EXCEL Program in British Columbia (with Vancouver Whitecaps FC) and Ontario.

CANADA RECORDS

"A" RECORDS	MP	MS	MIN	G	A
2017 CANADA	1	0	19		
2018 CANADA	0	0	0		
2019 CANADA	8	3	318		2a
2020 CANADA	6	6	399	1g	3a
2021 CANADA	11	5	567		
2022 CANADA	10	9	612		
2023 CANADA	7	5	430		
FIRST 7 YEARS	**43**	**28**	**2345**	**1g**	**5a**

FIFA / OLYMPIC	MP	MS	MIN	G	A
2019 FIFA WC	3	1	102		
2021 OLYMPIC	4	2	218		
2023 FIFA WC	3	3	205		

2021 OLYMPIC GAMES • Jayde Riviere made four appearances at the 2021 Olympic Football Tournament when Canada won a historic Gold Medal in Japan. Still only 20 years old at the time, she featured as a late substitute in the Quarterfinals, missed the Semifinals through suspension, and featured in extra time in the Final.

FORWARD

10

JODI-ANN ROBINSON

Born: 1989-04-17, St-Ann Bay, JAM. Grew up in Richmond, BC, CAN. Height 163 cm. Dominant right foot.

2 FIFA World Cups: Group phase in 2007 and 2011
1 Olympic Games: Quarterfinals at Beijing 2008
2 Concacaf medals: Silver in 2006 and 2008
1st #CANWNT: 2005-04-21 at Osnabrück, GER (v. GER)
1st Goal: 2006-10-28 at Seoul, KOR (v. ITA)

INTERNATIONAL CAREER

Jodi-Ann Robinson represented Canada at two FIFA youth tournaments, two FIFA World Cups and one Olympic Games. She helped Canada win Concacaf youth titles in 2004 and 2008 and she graduated as Canada's second-best youth goalscorer behind only Christine Sinclair.

As a teenager, Robinson was Canada's youngest player at the 2007 FIFA World Cup and their second-youngest player at the 2008 Olympic Games. They reached the Quarterfinals in 2008 before they were eliminated by the Americans in extra time.

In all, Robinson made 56 international "A" appearances for Canada across 10 years. She was just 16 years old when she made her Canada debut as a late substitute in Canada's 3-1 away loss to Germany on 21 April 2005.

CLUB CAREER

Robinson played club football in Canada, USA, Sweden and Norway. As a teenager, she won the USL W-League Championship with Vancouver Whitecaps FC in 2006. She then helped the Western New York Flash win the NWSL Shield in 2013, the league's inaugural season.

Before her pro career, she played college soccer at the University of West Florida.

CANADA RECORDS

"A" RECORDS	MP	MS	MIN	G	A
2004 CANADA	0	0	0		
2005 CANADA	3	1	89		
2006 CANADA	4	0	49	1g	
2007 CANADA	9	3	401	1g	
2008 CANADA	17	2	511	4g	1a
2009 CANADA	3	2	154		
2010 CANADA	6	6	393		2a
2011 CANADA	9	1	197	1g	
2012 CANADA	0	0	0		
2013 CANADA	5	3	209		
10 SEASONS	**56**	**18**	**2003**	**7g**	**3a**

FIFA / OLYMPIC	MP	MS	MIN	G	A
2007 FIFA WC	3	0	75		
2008 OLYMPIC	3	0	80		
2011 FIFA WC	1	0	6		

● ● ●

2007 FIFA WORLD CUP • Jodi-Ann Robinson made four appearances across back-to-back FIFA World Cups at China 2007 and Germany 2011. She was Canada's youngest player in 2007 when she came off the bench in all three group matches. She made her FIFA World Cup debut in the opener against former champions Norway.

DEANNE ROSE

WINGER / F

Born: 1999-03-03, Alliston, ON, CAN. Height 162 cm. Dominant right foot.

2 FIFA World Cups: France 2019, AU NZ 2023
2 Olympic Games: Bronze at Rio 2016, Gold at Tokyo in 2021
4 Concacaf medals: Silver in 2016, 2018, 2020, 2022
1st #CANWNT: 2015-12-09 at Natal, BRA (v. MEX)
1st Goal: 2016-02-11 OQ at Houston, TX, USA (v. GUY)

OLYMPIC CHAMPION

Deanne Rose has already represented Canada at two FIFA youth tournaments, two FIFA World Cups and two Olympic Games. She was Canada Soccer's U-17 Player of the Year in 2016.

She won an Olympic Bronze Medal in 2016 and an Olympic Gold Medal in 2021.

Rose co-led Canada with three assists in the short 2020 season and then helped Canada set a program record with a 12-match undefeated streak in 2021 (including the Olympic Gold Medal in Tokyo).

At Rio 2016, she featured in five Canada matches and made two starts. In the Bronze Medal match, she scored the first goal and got an assist on the second goal scored by Christine Sinclair.

LEICESTER CITY FC

Rose joined Leicester City FC ahead of the 2023-24 FA Women's Super League. She previously spent her first two pro seasons with Reading FC.

She made her professional debut with Reading FC on 12 September 2021.

Before turning pro, Rose played her college soccer at the University of Florida. As a teenager, she played for Scarborough GS United SC. She was the Top Scorer at Canada Soccer's National Championships in 2015.

CANADA RECORDS

"A" RECORDS	MP	MS	MIN	G	A
2015 CANADA	3	1	114		1a
2016 CANADA	16	10	870	4g	3a
2017 CANADA	11	9	637	3g	1a
2018 CANADA	5	1	73	1g	
2019 CANADA	8	3	250		
2020 CANADA	5	3	251	1g	3a
2021 CANADA	17	9	813	1g	
2022 CANADA	8	4	417		1a
2023 CANADA	4	1	129	1g	
FIRST 9 YEARS	77	41	3554	11g	9a

FIFA / OLYMPIC	MP	MS	MIN	G	A
2016 OLYMPIC	5	2	194	1g	1a
2019 FIFA WC	1	0	15		
2021 OLYMPIC	6	1	229		
2023 FIFA WC	2	1	90		

2021 OLYMPIC GAMES • Deanne Rose featured in all six matches when Canada won their historic Gold Medal at the 2021 Olympic Football Tournament in Japan. She came off the bench in five of those six matches including the Final when Canada beat Sweden on kicks from the penalty mark. Rose scored Canada's second goal in the shootout.

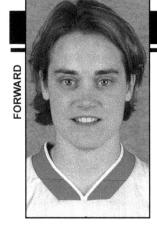

FORWARD

11

SHANNON ROSENOW

Born: 1972-06-20, Edmonton, AB, CAN.   Height 163 cm.
Dominant right foot.

1 FIFA World Cup: Group phase at USA 1999
1 Concacaf medal: Gold in 1998
1st #CANWNT: 1996-05-12 at Worcester, MA, USA (v. USA)
1st Goal: 1998-07-19 FWCQ at Ottawa, ON, CAN (v. CHN)

CONCACAF CHAMPION

Shannon Rosenow represented Canada at the 1999 FIFA World Cup less than a year after winning the Concacaf Championship in 1998. In the Concacaf Final, she set up Liz Smith for the 1-0 match winner against Mexico at Centennial Stadium in Toronto.

Rosenow scored seven goals for Canada at the 1998 Concacaf Championship, second most on the team behind Silvana Burtini.

Less than a month before the FIFA World Cup, Rosenow scored twice in a 3-0 win over Mexico at Burnaby. They were the last two international goals of her career.

At the FIFA World Cup in 1999, Rosenow started all three matches in the group phase against Japan, Norway and Russia.

In all, Rosenow made 28 appearances for Canada from 1996 to 2000. She was 23 years old when she made her debut on 12 May 1996 in a loss to the United States. Four years later, she played her last three matches in Portugal at the 2000 Algarve Cup (including a 3-2 win over Denmark on 18 March 2000).

CLUB CAREER

Rosenow played her club soccer in Canada where she won three national titles in six years with the Edmonton Angels (1995, 1999, 2000). She scored seven goals across those three tournaments.

She also played for the University of Alberta where she was coached by former Canada international Tracy David. Rosenow was a CIAU Second Team All-Canadian in 1992. She earned team MVP honours in 1994.

CANADA RECORDS

"A" RECORDS	MP	MS	MIN	G	A
1996 CANADA	3	1	106		
1997 CANADA	3	2	205		
1998 CANADA	8	8	637	9g	3a
1999 CANADA	11	10	774	2g	3a
2000 CANADA	3	2	156		
5 SEASONS	28	23	1878	11g	6a

FIFA / OLYMPIC	MP	MS	MIN	G	A
1999 FIFA WC	3	3	240		

● ● ●

1998 CONCACAF CHAMPIONSHIP • Shannon Rosenow set up Canada's title-winning goal at the Concacaf Championship in 1998, a Liz Smith 1-0 match winner at sold-out Centennial Stadium in Toronto. Rosenow's cross from the right in the 42nd minute was headed by Smith past Mexican goalkeeper Linnea Quinones.

12

CATHY ROSS

CENTRE BACK / RB

Born: 1967-11-19, New Westminster, BC, CAN. Grew up in Coquitlam, BC, CAN. Height 175 cm. Dominant right foot.

1 FIFA International Tournament: Quarterfinals at China 1988
1 FIFA World Cup: Group phase at Sweden 1995
1 Concacaf medal: Silver in 1991
1st #CANWNT: 1986-07-07 at Blaine, MN, USA (v. USA)
1st Goal: 1988-06-03 at Foshan, CHN (v. CIV)

CANADA SOCCER HALL OF FAME

Cathy Ross represented Canada at their first FIFA World Cup in 1995 after featuring at both the World Invitational Tournament in 1987 and FIFA's International Football Tournament in 1988. She left the program after winning Silver at the 1991 Concacaf Championship, but returned to the team in 1995 in the build up to the FIFA World Cup.

One of Canada's original Women's National Team members from 1986, she was the only player that featured in all 24 Canada "A" matches from 1986 to 1991. When she left international football for a second time in 1995, she ranked tied for fourth all time with 34 career appearances for Canada.

At the 1988 FIFA tournament, she played every minute of Canada's four matches including a narrow 1-0 loss to Sweden in the Quarterfinals. She scored in both the win against Côte d'Ivoire as well as the draw with the Netherlands.

Ross played her club football in Canada where she helped Coquitlam United SC win the 1987 National Championships for the Jubilee Trophy. She won provincial titles in both British Columbia (Coquitlam United) and Alberta (Edmonton Angels).

She played her college soccer at Simon Fraser University. She was a NAIA Second Team All-American in 1989.

CANADA RECORDS

"A" RECORDS		MP	MS	MIN	G	A
1986	CANADA	2	2	180		
1987	CANADA	8	8	600		
1988	CANADA	4	4	320	2g	
1989	CANADA	0	0	0		
1990	CANADA	5	5	400	1g	
1991	CANADA	5	5	360		
1995	CANADA	10	8	701		
7 SEASONS		**34**	**32**	**2561**	**3g**	

FIFA / OLYMPIC		MP	MS	MIN	G	A
1988	FIFA	4	4	320	2g	
1995	FIFA WC	2	2	168		

1995 FIFA WORLD CUP • Cathy Ross was one of six original members on Canada Soccer's Women's National Team in 1986 that also participated in Canada's first FIFA Women's World Cup at Sweden 1995. A centre back for most of her career, she came out of retirement and switched to right back for the 1995 FIFA World Cup.

MIDFIELDER / CB

CLARE RUSTAD

Born: 1983-05-27, North Vancouver, BC, CAN. Grew up in Salt Spring Island, BC, CAN. Height 178 cm. Dominant right foot.

1 Olympic Games: Quaterfinals at Beijing 2008
2 Concacaf medals: Silver in 2002 and 2008
1st #CANWNT: 2000-06-26 at Hershey, PA, USA (v. CHN)
1st Goal: 2003-09-04 at Burnaby, BC, CAN (v. MEX)

INTERNATIONAL CAREER

Clare Rustad won a FIFA Silver Medal at the inaugural FIFA U-19 Women's World Championship in Edmonton in 2002. She represented Canada at the Olympic Games six years later in Beijing.

With the National Team, she made her first 20 appearances as a teenager, then scored her first international goal as a substitute in Canada's second-last match before the 2003 FIFA World Cup. She was ultimately one of the last few cuts from the team ahead of the tournament.

More than four years later, Rustad returned to the squad and featured in 21 of Canada's 24 international matches including the Concacaf Olympic Qualifiers (second place) and the Beijing 2008 Olympic Games (they reached the Quarterfinals).

CLUB CAREER

Rustad played her club football in Canada, the United States and England. She helped Vancouver Whitecaps FC win the USL W-League Championship in 2004, but missed their title run in 2006 when she was away completing a Masters Degree in Epidemiology from the University of Cambridge.

In the United States, she played her college soccer at the University of Washington. She played her youth soccer on Vancouver Island.

She was honoured by the Soccer Hall of Fame of British Columbia in 2022.

CANADA RECORDS

"A" RECORDS		MP	MS	MIN	G	A
2000	CANADA	5	3	372		
2001	CANADA	5	2	xx		
2002	CANADA	9	7	658		
2003	CANADA	5	3	310	1g	
2008	CANADA	21	16	1577	2g	2a
2009	CANADA	0	0	0		
6 SEASONS		45	31	2917	3g	2a

FIFA / OLYMPIC		MP	MS	MIN	G	A
2008	OLYMPIC	4	4	390		1a

● ● ●

2008 OLYMPIC GAMES • Clare Rustad featured in every Canada minute at the Olympic Football Tournament in 2008 before they were eliminated by the Americans in extra time. In that Quarterfinals classic, Rustad caused the turnover that set up Christine Sinclair for her iconic 1-1 equaliser in the first half.

MIDFIELDER

⑥

ANITA SAIKO

Née Anita Brand. Born: 1961-10-23, Edmonton, AB, CAN. Grew up in Nelson, BC, CAN & Edmonton. Height 170 cm. Dominant right foot.

#CANWNT original selection in 1986

CANADA CAREER

Anita Saiko was an original selection for Canada's first Women's National Team in 1986, but she ultimately did not travel from Winnipeg for the North America Cup in Blaine, Minnesota. Saiko was one of 25 players selected from Canada Soccer's Women's All-Star Championship on 1 July 1986. She was considered one of the best players in the country in the 1980s.

CLUB CAREER

Saiko played her club football in Canada where she won a joint-record six National Championships from 1982 to 1988 with the Edmonton Angels. Saiko and Tracy David won six titles in that span, including the first five National Championships from 1982 to 1986. Goalkeeper Sue Simon joined their exclusive club when she won her sixth title in 1995.

Saiko, née Anita Brand, won five of those six titles playing alongside her younger sister, Sue Brand. Anita and Sue were teammates when they lifted the Jubilee Trophy together in 1983, 1984, 1985, 1986 and 1988. The

Angels finished in third place in the country in 1987. They won seven-straight Alberta provincial titles from 1982 to 1988.

Saiko won her first national title in her first season with the Angels. Before she joined the club, she spent her first two seasons in the Edmonton First Division with the Edmonton Blazers and she was the league's top scorer as a teenager in 1980.

Growing up, she played her youth soccer in Edmonton, Alberta and Nelson, British Columbia. Her father Joe played in the old Edmonton First Division as well as the Western Canada Soccer League.

CANADA RECORDS

"A" RECORDS	MP	MS	MIN	G	A
1986 CANADA	-	-	-		

WOMEN'S ALL-STAR CHAMPIONSHIP • Canada Soccer's first Women's National Team selection camp in July 1986 followed the inaugural eight-team Women's All-Star Championship in Winnipeg. Canada Soccer's Head Coach Neil Turnbull picked 25 players from the All-Star Championship including Alberta's Anita Saiko.

MIDFIELDER / CB

SOPHIE SCHMIDT

Born: 1988-06-28, Winnipeg, MB, CAN. Grew up in Abbotsford, BC, CAN. Height 172 cm. Dominant right foot.

5 FIFA World Cups: 2007, 2011, 2015, 2019, 2023
4 Olympic Games: QF 2008, Bronze 2012, 2016, Gold 2021
8 Concacaf: Gold 2010, Silver 2006, '08, '12, '16, '18, '20, '22
1st #CANWNT: 2005-04-19 at Apeldoorn, NED (v. NED)
1st Goal: 2005-04-27 at Bischheim, FRA (v. FRA)

OLYMPIC CHAMPION

Sophie Schmidt has already represented Canada at two FIFA youth tournaments, five FIFA World Cups and four Olympic Games. She set the Canada record with 76 consecutive appearances from 2011 to 2015.

She left international football at the end of 2023 ranked second on Canada with 226 career appearances. She played in every Canada match at five-straight FIFA World Cups from 2007 to 2023.

She also played every Canada match at three Olympic Games from 2008 to 2016. At London 2012, she got three assists and was part of the build up on the iconic goal by Diana Matheson.

HOUSTON DASH

Schmidt joined the Houston Dash in 2019 and helped the club win the Challenge Cup in 2020. She has played her club football in Canada, USA and Germany. She won the USL W-League Championship in 2006. With FFC Frankfurt, she reached the UEFA Champions League Semifinals in 2015-16.

CANADA RECORDS

"A" RECORDS		MP	MS	MIN	G	A
2005	CANADA	10	10	885	1g	
2006	CANADA	11	6	538	1g	
2007	CANADA	5	4	371	1g	
2008	CANADA	17	15	1269		
2009	CANADA	0	0	0		
2010	CANADA	7	6	570		
2011	CANADA	24	21	1944		
2012	CANADA	22	20	1732	4g	7a
2013	CANADA	17	16	1265	2g	3a
2014	CANADA	11	11	913	6g	2a
2015	CANADA	13	13	1082	1g	
2016	CANADA	20	15	1321	1g	3a
2017	CANADA	7	7	582	1g	
2018	CANADA	12	9	855		4a
2019	CANADA	15	13	1195	1g	
2020	CANADA	8	8	658		
2021	CANADA	10	4	404		
2022	CANADA	9	0	206	1g	2a
2023	CANADA	8	1	326	1g	2a
18 SEASONS		**226**	**179**	**16116**	**20g**	**22a**

FIFA / OLYMPIC		MP	MS	MIN	G	A
2007	FIFA WC	3	3	270	1g	
2008	OLYMPIC	4	4	345		
2011	FIFA WC	3	3	270		
2012	OLYMPIC	6	6	556		3a
2015	FIFA WC	5	5	441		
2016	OLYMPIC	6	4	370	1g	
2019	FIFA WC	4	4	360		
2021	OLYMPIC	1	1	90		
2023	FIFA WC	3	0	109		1a

● ● ●

2016 OLYMPIC GAMES • Sophie Schmidt featured in all six matches when Canada won their second Olympic Bronze Medal in 2016. In the group phase, she earned Player of the Match honours in the 3-1 win over Zimbabwe. In the Quarterfinals, she scored the 1-0 match winner and earned Player of the Match honours against France.

MIDFIELDER

DESIREE SCOTT

Born: 1987-07-31, Winnipeg, MB, CAN. Height 155 cm. Dominant right foot.

3 FIFA World Cups: 2011, 2015, 2019
3 Olympic Games: Bronze 2012, 2016, Gold 2021
5 Concacaf medals: Gold 2010, Silver 2012, 2016, 2020, 2022
1st #CANWNT: 2010-02-24 at Larnaka, CYP (v. POL)

OLYMPIC CHAMPION

Desiree Scott has already represented Canada at one FIFA youth tournament, three FIFA World Cups and three Olympic Games. She missed the 2023 FIFA World Cup through injury.

Scott won an Olympic Gold Medal in 2021 after winning back-to-back Olympic Bronze Medals in 2012 and 2016. She also won a Gold Medal at the 2011 Pan American Games.

While she played her first few international matches in an attacking role, she cemented herself as one of the world's best defensive midfielders. In 2022, she moved into fourth place on Canada's all-time list for career international appearances.

KANSAS CITY CURRENT

Scott has played her football in Canada, USA and England. She featured in the NWSL's inaugural season in 2013 with FC Kansas City and she featured in the 2015 FA Cup Final at Wembley when Notts County FC were runners up.

Scott helped the Kansas City Current reach the NWSL Final in 2022. That season, she was a recipient of the NWSLPA Ally Award.

CANADA RECORDS

"A" RECORDS		MP	MS	MIN	G	A
2009	CANADA	0	0	0		
2010	CANADA	10	3	448		
2011	CANADA	22	7	943		
2012	CANADA	21	21	1900		
2013	CANADA	17	14	1230		
2014	CANADA	11	6	676		
2015	CANADA	18	14	1244		1a
2016	CANADA	18	18	1438		1a
2017	CANADA	12	10	917		
2018	CANADA	6	6	448		
2019	CANADA	13	13	1075		
2020	CANADA	8	6	554		2a
2021	CANADA	14	13	1186		
2022	CANADA	15	13	974		
2023	CANADA	INJ				
FIRST 15 YEARS		185	144	13033		4a

FIFA / OLYMPIC		MP	MS	MIN	G	A
2011	FIFA WC	2	0	42		
2012	OLYMPIC	6	6	570		
2015	FIFA WC	5	4	340		
2016	OLYMPIC	5	5	434		1a
2019	FIFA WC	4	4	349		
2021	OLYMPIC	5	5	509		

2012 OLYMPIC GAMES • Midfielder Desiree Scott featured in every Canada minute when they won their inspiring Bronze Medal at the London 2012 Olympic Football Tournament. "The Destroyer" was a force against the Americans in the Semifinals and she made a memorable goal-line block against France in Canada's final match of the tournament.

FORWARD

CARRIE SERWETNYK

Born: 1965-07-17, Hamilton, ON, CAN. Grew up in Mississauga, ON, CAN. Height 165 cm.

1 FIFA International Tournament: Quarterfinals at China 1988
1 Concacaf medal: Silver in 1991
1st #CANWNT: 1986-07-07 at Blaine, MN, USA (v. USA)
1st Goal: 1990-07-27 at Winnipeg, MB, CAN (v. USA)

CANADA SOCCER HALL OF FAME

Carrie Serwetnyk represented Canada at both the World Invitational Tournament in 1987 and FIFA's International Football Tournament in 1988. She won Silver at the first Concacaf Championship in 1991.

One of Canada's original Women's National Team players from 1986, Serwetnyk scored the program's first home international goal when they hosted their first two matches at Winnipeg in 1990.

Across 11 years, she made 18 international "A" appearances for Canada. She played her last Canada match on 18 May 1996 in a 0-0 draw with Japan at Washington.

Serwetnyk played club football in Canada, the United States, France and Japan. She won Japan's L.League with Yomiuri SC Beleza in 1993.

Serwetnyk played her college soccer in the United States where she won three NCAA College Cups with the University of North Carolina (1984, 1986, 1987).

She won back-to-back Women's All-Star Championships with Ontario in 1986 and 1987.

As a youth player, she helped Clarkson Sheridan reach Canada Soccer's U-18 Cup Final in 1982.

CANADA RECORDS

"A" RECORDS	MP	MS	MIN	G	A
1986 CANADA	1	1	90		
1987 CANADA	7	3	xx		
1988 CANADA	1	0	32		
1990 CANADA	2	1	xx	1g	
1991 CANADA	4	2	190		
1996 CANADA	3	0	68		
6 SEASONS	**18**	**7**	**n/a**	**1g**	

FIFA / OLYMPIC	MP	MS	MIN	G	A
1988 FIFA	1	0	32		

● ● ●

1988 FIFA INTERNATIONAL TOURNAMENT • Carrie Serwetnyk made one appearance at FIFA's first women's international tournament in June 1988. She came on as a substitute in the second half of Canada's second group match, a 6-0 win over Côte d'Ivoire. Canada went on to reach the Quarterfinals, but they were eliminated after a narrow 1-0 loss to Sweden.

10

LAUREN SESSELMANN

LEFT BACK / CB

Born: 1983-08-14, Stevens Point, WI, USA. Grew up in Green Bay, WI, USA. Height 173 cm. Dominant left foot.

1 FIFA World Cup: Quarterfinals at Canada 2015
1 Olympic Games: Bronze at London 2012
1 Concacaf medal: Silver in 2012
1st #CANWNT: 2011-09-17 at Kansas City, KS, USA (v. USA)

OLYMPIC BRONZE MEDAL

Lauren Sesselmann won a Bronze Medal at the London 2012 Olympic Games and then reached the Quarterfinals at Canada's home FIFA World Cup in 2015. She also won a Gold Medal at the Pan American Games in 2011.

Across five years from 2011 to 2015, she made 46 career international appearances for Canada. She made her Canada debut against the Americans in Head Coach John Herdman's first match in charge.

At the Pan American Games Guadalajara 2011, she set up Robyn Gayle for the late 2-1 match winner in their Semifinals victory over Colombia.

CLUB CAREER

Sesselmann played her club football in the United States where she helped FC Indiana win the 2007 WPSL Championship and then reach the 2008 USL W-League Final.

She then played her pro soccer in the WPS and NWSL. In 2013 with FC Kansas City,

she helped her team finish second in the standings before they were eliminated in the playoff semifinals. She was named to the league's Second XI.

She played her college soccer at Purdue University where she was a two-time First Team All-Big Ten selection (2003, 2005).

CANADA RECORDS

"A" RECORDS	MP	MS	MIN	G	A
2011 CANADA	8	7	533		1a
2012 CANADA	18	17	1353		2a
2013 CANADA	13	11	930		1a
2014 CANADA	1	1	90		
2015 CANADA	6	6	449		
5 SEASONS	46	42	3355		4a

FIFA / OLYMPIC	MP	MS	MIN	G	A
2012 OLYMPIC	6	6	550		1a
2015 FIFA WC	4	4	338		

2012 OLYMPIC GAMES • Lauren Sesselmann featured in all six matches when Canada won their inspiring Olympic Bronze Medal at London 2012. She started at left back, but mostly played centre back to cover for injuries. In their last match against France, she won the initial interception that led to Diana Matheson's iconic match winner in the final minute.

GOALKEEPER

1

KAILEN SHERIDAN

Born: 1995-07-16, Pickering, ON, CAN. Grew up in Whitby, ON, CAN. Height 177 cm. Dominant right foot.

2 FIFA World Cups: France 2019, AU NZ 2023
1 Olympic Games: Gold at Tokyo in 2021
3 Concacaf medals: Silver in 2018, 2020, 2022
1st #CANWNT: 2016-03-07 at Lagos, POR (v. ISL)
1st Goal: 2016-03-07 at Lagos, POR (v. ISL)

OLYMPIC CHAMPION

Kailen Sheridan has already represented Canada at two FIFA youth tournaments, two FIFA World Cups and one Olympic Games. She was also an alternate at the Rio 2016 Olympic Games.

In 2021, she helped Canada set a program record with a 12-match undefeated streak, including their historic Olympic Gold Medal.

In 2016, Sheridan posted her first clean sheet in her Canada debut against Iceland. In 2022, she posted a career-best eight clean sheets in 15 matches.

She made her Olympic debut in 2021 and her FIFA World Cup debut in 2023.

SAN DIEGO WAVE FC

Sheridan helped San Diego Wave FC win the 2023 NWSL Shield after they finished in first place in the league standings. She was named to the NWSL's Best XI in 2022 and the Second XI in 2023. As an expansion club, they finished in third place in the 2022 standings.

Before joining San Diego, Sheridan played for NJ/NY Gotham FC. She won the NWSL Challenge Cup Golden Glove award in 2020 and was named to the NWSL's Best XI in 2021.

Before turning pro, she played her college soccer at Clemson University.

CANADA RECORDS

"A" RECORDS		MP	MS	MIN		CS
2016	CANADA	1	1	90	1	CS
2017	CANADA	3	2	180	1	CS
2018	CANADA	2	2	180	2	CS
2019	CANADA	1	1	90	1	CS
2020	CANADA	2	2	180	1	CS
2021	CANADA	7	5	446	2	CS
2022	CANADA	15	14	1213	8	CS
2023	CANADA	12	11	1050	5	CS
FIRST 9 YEARS		43	38	3429	21	CS

FIFA / OLYMPIC		MP	MS	MIN		CS
2016	OLYMPIC	-	-	-		
2019	FIFA WC	0	0	0		
2021	OLYMPIC	2	1	122	0	CS
2023	FIFA WC	3	3	270	1	CS

● ● ●

2022 CONCACAF CHAMPIONSHIP • Goalkeeper Kailen Sheridan won the Golden Glove as the Best Goalkeeper at the 2022 Concacaf Women's Championship when Canada qualified for the 2023 FIFA World Cup. She posted three clean sheets and conceded only one goal to the Americans on a penalty kick.

21

SUE SIMON

Born: 1961-07-05, Edmonton, AB, CAN. Height 170 cm. Dominant right foot.

1st #CANWNT: 1986-07-07 at Blaine, MN, USA (v. USA)

GOALKEEPER

CANADA SOCCER HALL OF FAME

Sue Simon was Canada's first goalkeeper when the Women's National Team made their international debut at the 1986 North America Cup in Blaine, Minnesota. Canada lost the first match 2-0 to the Americans, but won the second match 2-1 just two days later on Wednesday 9 July.

Simon played both the 1986 and 1987 North America Cups alongside goalkeeping teammate Carla Chin. They shared duties in 1987, with Simon in goal for the matches against Sweden and USA.

After those four international matches in 1986 and 1987, she sat out the 1988 and 1989 seasons with the birth of her two boys.

Simon played her club football in Canada where she won a joint record six National Championships with the Edmonton Angels. Simon won five-straight titles from 1982 to 1986, then won her sixth title in 1995.

She was just the third six-time winner after teammates Tracy David and Anita Saiko both won their sixth titles with the Angels in 1988. David and Saiko were retired before Simon and the Angels won their seventh national title in 1995.

As a goalkeeper, Simon held the National Championships all-time record for clean sheets. In Edmonton's First Division, she sometimes played out of goal and was in fact a league all-star as an outfield player in 1980 when she played for Edmonton Dominco Gold (defender/midfielder).

Before joining the Angels in 1982, Simon won the 1981 Edmonton First Division title with Edmonton Ajax. With the Angels, she was part of seven of their nine city titles from 1982 to 1990.

CANADA RECORDS

"A" RECORDS	MP	MS	MIN		CS
1986 CANADA	2	2	180	0	CS
1987 CANADA	2	2	180	0	CS
2 SEASONS	**4**	**4**	**360**	**0**	**CS**

1986 NORTH AMERICA CUP • Goalkeeper Sue Simon was Canada's Most Valuable Player when they posted their first-ever international win at the 1986 North America Cup in Blaine, Minnesota. Just two days after a 2-0 loss, Simon helped Canada win 2-1 over the Americans in the second match of the series on Wednesday 9 July 1986.

FORWARD

CHRISTINE SINCLAIR

Born: 1983-06-12, Burnaby, BC, CAN. Height 175 cm.

6 FIFA World Cups: 2003, 2007, 2011, 2015, 2019, 2023
4 Olympic Games: 2008, Bronze 2012, 2016, Gold 2021
10 Concacaf medals: Gold 2010, Silver 2002, 2006, 2008, 2012, 2016, 2018, 2020, 2022, Bronze 2004
1st #CANWNT: 2000-03-12 at Lagoa, POR (v. CHN)
1st Goal: 2000-03-14 at Albufeira, POR (v. NOR)

OLYMPIC CHAMPION

Christine Sinclair represented Canada in one FIFA youth tournament, six FIFA World Cups and four Olympic Games. She won the Concacaf Championship in 2010, a Pan American Games Gold Medal in 2011, back-to-back Olympic Bronze Medals in 2012 and 2016, and an Olympic Gold Medal in 2021.

She left international football at the end of 2023 ranked first in the world in goals (190) and second in career appearances (331). She played in every Canada match at six-straight FIFA World Cups from 2003 to 2023.

She set a Canada record with 23 goals scored in 2012, including a hat trick against the Americans in the unforgettable London 2012 Semifinals at Old Trafford.

PORTLAND THORNS FC

Since turning pro in 2009, Sinclair has won five playoff titles in the United States: two in the WPS (2010, 2011) and three in the NWSL (2013, 2017, 2022). She was MVP of the 2011 WPS Championship, co-led the WPS in goalscoring once (2011), and led the league in assists twice (2010, 2011).

In 2013, she was an original member of Portland Thorns FC in the inaugural NWSL season.

CANADA RECORDS

"A" RECORDS	MP	MS	MIN	G	A
2000 CANADA	18	17	1599	15g	
2001 CANADA	12	12	1080	6g	
2002 CANADA	10	10	904	11g	4a
2003 CANADA	17	16	1461	11g	3a
2004 CANADA	9	9	810	6g	
2005 CANADA	7	7	628	4g	
2006 CANADA	17	17	1513	13g	4a
2007 CANADA	13	12	1063	16g	3a
2008 CANADA	22	22	2017	13g	2a
2009 CANADA	7	7	626	4g	1a
2010 CANADA	16	15	1387	13g	7a
2011 CANADA	20	19	1810	8g	4a
2012 CANADA	22	22	1950	23g	6a
2013 CANADA	13	13	1170	4g	1a
2014 CANADA	11	11	990	1g	1a
2015 CANADA	18	18	1578	10g	4a
2016 CANADA	18	15	1293	7g	4a
2017 CANADA	12	11	960	4g	6a
2018 CANADA	12	11	979	8g	2a
2019 CANADA	15	14	1208	6g	1a
2020 CANADA	7	7	517	3g	
2021 CANADA	12	12	886	2g	
2022 CANADA	11	10	651	2g	2a
2023 CANADA	12	6	521		
23 SEASONS	**331**	**313**	**27,601**	**190g**	**55a**

FIFA / OLYMPIC	MP	MS	MIN	G	A
2003 FIFA WC	6	6	540	3g	1a
2007 FIFA WC	3	3	270	3g	1a
2008 OLYMPIC	4	4	367	2g	
2011 FIFA WC	3	3	270	1g	
2012 OLYMPIC	6	6	568	6g	1a
2015 FIFA WC	5	5	450	2g	1a
2016 OLYMPIC	5	5	450	3g	1a
2019 FIFA WC	4	4	338	1g	
2021 OLYMPIC	5	5	466	1g	
2023 FIFA WC	3	1	161		

2

LIZ SMITH

MIDFIELDER

Born: 1975-09-25, Edmonton, AB, CAN. Height 170 cm. Dominant right foot.

1 FIFA World Cup: Group phase at USA 1999
1 Concacaf medal: Gold in 1998
1st #CANWNT: 1996-05-15 at New Britain, CT, USA (v. CHN)
1st Goal: 1998-08-30 FWCQ at Toronto, ON, CAN (v. MTQ)

CONCACAF CHAMPION

Liz Smith represented Canada at the 1999 FIFA World Cup after winning the Concacaf Championship in 1998. She was the hero in the Concacaf Final after she scored the 1-0 match winner against Mexico

With Canada from 1996 to 2000, Smith made 22 international "A" appearances and scored both of her goals at the Concacaf Championship (she also scored against Martinique in the group phase). She played in 16 consecutive Canada matches from 1996 to 1999.

She made her Canada debut in a 5-0 loss to China PR in 1996. She played her last match in 2000 at the Pacific Cup in Australia, a 2-2 draw with the FIFA World Cup runners up China PR.

CLUB CAREER

Smith played her club football in Canada and Germany. From 1995 to 2000, she helped the Edmonton Angels win Canada Soccer's National Championships three times in six years (1995, 1999, 2000).

In between her run of titles, Smith played in the German Bundesliga for FFC Heike Rheine ahead of the 1999 FIFA World Cup with her Canada teammate Tanya Franck.

She played college soccer at the University of Alberta where she was coached by Tracy David, a former Canada player. After they were CIAU runners up in 1996, they lifted the Gladys Bean Memorial Trophy as national champions in 1997.

In 1994, she helped Alberta's U-19 team win the youth all-star championship.

CANADA RECORDS

"A" RECORDS	MP	MS	MIN	G	A
1996 CANADA	4	4	360		
1997 CANADA	3	3	225		
1998 CANADA	8	8	685	2g	1a
1999 CANADA	4	3	144		
2000 CANADA	3	1	165		
5 SEASONS	22	19	1579	2g	1a

FIFA / OLYMPIC	MP	MS	MIN	G	A
1999 FIFA WC	0	0	0		

1998 CONCACAF CHAMPIONSHIP • Liz Smith scored Canada's title-winning goal when they beat Mexico in the 1998 Concacaf Championship Final. In front of a sold-out, record-setting crowd, Smith scored the 1-0 match winner from a header on a Shannon Rosenow cross in the 42nd minute at Toronto's Centennial Stadium (4,971 spectators).

FULLBACK / M

CHELSEA STEWART

Born: 1990-04-28, Denver, CO, USA. Grew up in Denver, CO, USA & The Pas, MB, CAN. Height 164 cm. Dominant right foot.

1 FIFA World Cup: Group phase at Germany 2011
1 Olympic Games: Bronze at London 2012
2 Concacaf medals: Gold in 2010, Silver in 2012
1st #CANWNT: 2009-03-05 at Paralimni, CYP (v. NZL)

OLYMPIC BRONZE MEDAL

Chelsea Stewart represented Canada at one FIFA youth tournament, one FIFA World Cup, and one Olympic Games. She won a Concacaf youth title in 2008 and was Canada Soccer's U-20 Player of the Year in 2009.

From late 2010 to early 2011, she helped Canada set a program record with an 11-match undefeated streak. Inside that streak, she helped Canada win the 2010 Concacaf Championship.

From 2008 to 2014, she made 44 career international "A" appearances with Canada. She was 18 years old when she made her debut on 5 March 2019 at the Cyprus Cup.

She made a career-high 14 appearances in 2012 when Canada won an Olympic Bronze Medal.

CLUB CAREER

Stewart played club football in the United States, Canada, Japan and Germany. She reached the USL W-League Final with Vancouver Whitecaps FC in 2010 when they lost to the Buffalo Flash.

Stewart played her college soccer in the United States at Vanderbilt University and UCLA. She won the NCAA College Cup with UCLA when they beat Florida State in the 2013 Final.

CANADA RECORDS

"A" RECORDS	MP	MS	MIN	G	A
2008 CANADA	0	0	0		
2009 CANADA	6	3	293		
2010 CANADA	11	3	370		
2011 CANADA	8	1	195		
2012 CANADA	14	2	395		
2013 CANADA	5	3	328		
2014 CANADA	0	0	0		
7 SEASONS	44	12	1581		

FIFA / OLYMPIC	MP	MS	MIN	G	A
2008 OLYMPIC	-	-	-		
2011 FIFA WC	1	0	13		
2012 OLYMPIC	4	0	65		

● ● ●

2012 OLYMPIC GAMES • Chelsea Stewart came off the bench to make four appearances at left back when Canada won their inspiring Bronze Medal at the London 2012 Olympic Football Tournament. Against South Africa, she was part of the sequence that led to Christine Sinclair's second goal in a 3-0 win at Coventry.

2

HELEN STOUMBOS

FORWARD

Born: 1970-10-18, Guelph, ON, CAN.　Height 158 cm. Dominant right foot.

1 FIFA World Cup: Group phase at Sweden 1995
3 Concacaf medals: Gold 1998, Silver 1994, Bronze 1993
1st #CANWNT: 1993-06-10 at Columbus, OH, USA (v. ITA)
1st Goal: 1995-06-06 FWC at Helsingborg, SWE (v. ENG)

CANADA SOCCER HALL OF FAME

Helen Stoumbos represented Canada at one FIFA World Cup and she won medals at three Concacaf tournaments in six years. After winning the Concacaf Championship in 1998, she missed the FIFA World Cup in 1999 because of a knee injury.

She was Canada's first goalscorer at the 1995 FIFA World Cup against England.

From 1993 to 1999, she made 35 career international "A" appearances, which at the time ranked sixth all time for Canada. She was 22 years old when she made her debut in a 4-0 loss to Italy on 10 June 1993.

Before winning a Concacaf title in 1998, Stoumbos featured in all three Canada matches at the 1993 Concacaf Invitational and then all four Canada matches at the 1994 Concacaf Championship. Canada qualified for their first FIFA World Cup when they beat Trinidad and Tobago in Montréal.

Stoumbos played her club football in both Canada and the United States. At the 1993

World University Games in Hamilton, she played for the Ontario Selects.

At Wilfrid Laurier University, she led her school to a CIAU Championship in 1992. She was a two-time CIAU First Team All-Canadian.

CANADA RECORDS

"A" RECORDS	MP	MS	MIN	G	A
1993 CANADA	6	3	341		
1994 CANADA	11	7	734		
1995 CANADA	11	9	833	1g	1a
1996 CANADA	5	4	321		
1998 CANADA	2	1	88		
1999 CANADA	0	0	0		
6 SEASONS	**35**	**24**	**2317**	**1g**	**1a**

FIFA / OLYMPIC	MP	MS	MIN	G	A
1995 FIFA WC	3	2	193	1g	
1999 FIFA WC	INJ	-	-		

1995 FIFA WORLD CUP • Helen Stoumbos scored Canada's first FIFA World Cup goal on an Olimpico, a right-footed corner kick that curled past Pauline Cope and the England defence in the 87th minute. It was Canada's first of two late goals in their first-ever FIFA Women's World Cup match, ultimately a 3-2 loss on 6 June 1995 at Helsingborg.

GOALKEEPER

TARYN SWIATEK

Born: 1981-02-04, Calgary, AB, CAN. Height 177 cm. Dominant right foot.

2 FIFA World Cups: 4th Place in 2003, Group phase in 2007
1 Concacaf medal: Bronze in 2004
1st #CANWNT: 2001-06-10 at Linköping, SWE (v. SWE)
1st Clean Sheet: 2003-05-19 at Lachine, QC, CAN (v. ENG)

INTERNATIONAL CAREER

Taryn Swiatek represented Canada at back-to-back FIFA World Cups and won medals at back-to-back Pan American Games. She backstopped Canada to a fourth place finish at the FIFA World Cup in 2003.

At age 22, she was Canada's youngest goalkeeper ever at a FIFA Women's World Cup.

In 2007, she helped the full National Team win Bronze at the Pan American Games. At the FIFA World Cup, she made her last international appearance against Australia.

From 2000 to 2007, she made 24 career international "A" appearances with Canada. She was just 20 years old when she made her debut on 10 June 2001 in a 5-2 away loss to Sweden.

CLUB CAREER

Swiatek played her club football in Canada and Denmark. She went on loan to Fortuna Hjørring at the end of the 2003-04 season and helped the team finish second in the league standings. The following year, she helped Ottawa Fury FC reach the 2005 USL W-League Final.

Swiatek played her college soccer at the University of Calgary. At the youth level, she won Canada Soccer's U-17 Cup with Calgary Celtic SFC in 1998. She also helped Alberta's U-18 team win a youth all-star championship that same year.

CANADA RECORDS

"A" RECORDS	MP	MS	MIN		CS
2000 CANADA	0	0	0		
2001 CANADA	3	3	270	0	CS
2002 CANADA	0	0	0		
2003 CANADA	8	6	592	4	CS
2004 CANADA	3	3	270	0	CS
2005 CANADA	4	3	315	0	CS
2006 CANADA	2	1	133	0	CS
2007 CANADA	4	3	236	1	CS
8 SEASONS	24	19	1816	5	CS

FIFA / OLYMPIC	MP	MS	MIN		CS
2003 FIFA WC	5	5	450	2	CS
2007 FIFA WC	1	0	11	0	CS

● ● ●

2003 FIFA WORLD CUP • Taryn Swiatek made six appearances across back-to-back FIFA World Cups at USA 2003 and China 2007. Just over a month after winning a Silver Medal with the U-23 squad at the 2003 Pan American Games, she played five of Canada's six matches at the FIFA World Cup including a 1-0 victory over China PR in the Quarterfinals.

14

MELISSA TANCREDI

FORWARD

Born: 1981-12-27, Hamilton, ON, CAN. Height 174 cm. Dominant right foot.

3 FIFA World Cups: 2007, 2011, Quarterfinals 2015
3 Olympic Games: 2008, Bronze 2012 and 2016
6 Concacaf: Gold 2010, Silver 2006, 2008, 2012, 2016, Bronze '04
1st #CANWNT: 2004-02-26 OQ at Herédia, CRC (v. JAM)
1st Goal: 2007-07-14 at Rio, BRA (v. URU)

OLYMPIC BRONZE MEDAL

Melissa Tancredi represented Canada at three FIFA World Cups and three Olympic Games. She scored the winning goals that qualified Canada for the Olympic Games in 2008 and 2012.

She won back-to-back Bronze Medals at the London 2012 and Rio 2016 Olympic Games.

Tancredi scored just 37 seconds into her FIFA World Cup debut which at the time was the second-fastest goal in a FIFA Women's World Cup match.

Across 14 international seasons from 2004 to 2017, Tancredi scored 27 goals in 125 career international "A" matches. She scored seven goals across three Olympic Games, including both goals in a 2-1 win over Germany at the 2016 Olympic Football Tournament in Brazil.

CLUB CAREER

Tancredi played her club football in Canada, the United States, and Sweden. In 2010,

she helped Vancouver Whitecaps FC reach the USL W-League Final. At the youth level, she won Canada Soccer's U-19 Cup with the Burlington Sting.

CANADA RECORDS

"A" RECORDS	MP	MS	MIN	G	A
2004 CANADA	7	6	487		
2005 CANADA	6	3	161		
2006 CANADA	1	1	33		
2007 CANADA	7	4	389	2g	
2008 CANADA	18	17	1283	6g	5a
2009 CANADA	4	1	185	1g	1a
2010 CANADA	9	9	674	2g	3a
2011 CANADA	15	13	1071	3g	2a
2012 CANADA	21	18	1648	8g	5a
2013 CANADA	1	1	61		
2014 CANADA	3	2	131		
2015 CANADA	17	11	876		1a
2016 CANADA	15	9	752	5g	2a
2017 CANADA	1	0	14		
14 SEASONS	**125**	**95**	**7765**	**27**	**19a**

FIFA / OLYMPIC	MP	MS	MIN	G	A
2007 FIFA WC	2	2	113	1g	
2008 OLYMPIC	3	3	177	1g	
2011 FIFA WC	3	2	194		
2012 OLYMPIC	6	6	554	4g	2a
2015 FIFA WC	5	4	336		
2016 OLYMPIC	5	5	328	2g	

2012 OLYMPIC GAMES • Melissa Tancredi scored four goals and two assists in six matches when Canada captured a Bronze Medal at the London 2012 Olympic Football Tournament. She scored in all three group matches, including a brace in Canada's come-from-behind 2-2 draw with Sweden in the group finale.

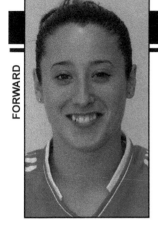

FORWARD

16

KATIE THORLAKSON

Born: 1985-01-14, New Westminster, BC, CAN. Grew up in Langley, BC, CAN. Height 158 cm. Dominant right foot.

1 FIFA World Cup: Group phase at China 2007
1st #CANWNT: 2004-07-30 at Tokyo, JPN (v. JPN)
1st Goal: 2007-07-18 at Rio, BRA (v. JAM)

INTERNATIONAL CAREER

Katie Thorlakson represented Canada at one FIFA youth tournament and one FIFA World Cup. After winning a FIFA Silver Medal at the inaugural FIFA U-19 World Championship in 2002, she helped Canada win the Concacaf Under-19 Championship in 2004.

In 2003, she helped the U-23 squad win a Silver Medal at the Pan American Games in Santo Domingo. In 2007, she helped the full National Team win Bronze at the next Pan American Games in Rio. She scored her first two international goals in an 11-1 win over Jamaica.

She was just 19 years old when she made her international debut in 3-0 loss to Japan on 30 July 2004 in Tokyo.

CLUB CAREER

Thorlakson played club football in Canada and Australia. She played for the Vancouver Whitecaps team that twice won the USL W-League Championship, but she missed the title match in 2004 because of school commitments and the 2006 Final through injury. She later won six-straight medals with Surrey United SC at Canada Soccer's National Championships, most notably gold and the Jubilee Trophy in 2011.

Thorlakson played her college soccer at the University of Notre Dame in the United States. She graduated as the school's all-time leading scorer.

She played her youth soccer in Langley, British Columbia.

CANADA RECORDS

"A" RECORDS	MP	MS	MIN	G	A
2004 CANADA	1	1	89		
2005 CANADA	8	5	494		
2006 CANADA	4	0	58		
2007 CANADA	10	9	721	2g	1a
4 SEASONS	23	15	1362	2g	1a

FIFA / OLYMPIC	MP	MS	MIN	G	A
2007 FIFA WC	1	1	44		

● ● ●

2007 FIFA WORLD CUP • Katie Thorlakson made one appearance at the FIFA Women's World Cup China 2007 when she started up front alongside Christine Sinclair and Kara Lang, the same trio that starred together as youth players in 2002. She was hurt late in the first half and missed the next match through injury.

17

BRITTANY TIMKO

FORWARD / FB

Born: 1985-09-05, Vancouver, BC, CAN. Grew up in Coquitlam, BC, CAN. Height 172 cm. Dominant right foot.

3 FIFA World Cups: 4th Place 2003, Group phase 2007, 2011
2 Olympic Games: Quaterfinals 2008, Bronze 2012
5 Concacaf medals: Silver 2002, 2006, 2008, 2012, Bronze 2004
1st #CANWNT: 2002-04-09 at Limoges, FRA (v. FRA)
1st Goal: 2008-06-14 at Suwon, KOR (v. ARG)

CANADA SOCCER HALL OF FAME

Brittany Timko won a Bronze Medal from two Olympic Games and featured in three FIFA World Cups as an international player. She retired ranked tied for fourth with 132 career international appearances.

She won a Silver Medal from the first FIFA U-19 World Championship in 2002 and then won the FIFA Golden Boot as the top scorer in the next edition at Thailand 2004.

She twice helped Canada set program records for undefeated streaks (2003 and 2010-11). In 2003, she featured in all six Canada matches as they finished fourth overall at the FIFA World Cup.

She was just 16 years old when she made her international debut on 9 April 2002 in a 3-2 loss to Japan.

At the club level, she played her football in Canada, the United States, Australia, Sweden and Germany. She won the USL W-League Championship in 2004 and 2006 with Vancouver Whitecaps FC.

She played her college soccer in the United States at the University of Nebraska. She was a three-time Big 12 Player of the Year.

Growing up, she played her youth soccer in Coquitam.

CANADA RECORDS

"A" RECORDS	MP	MS	MIN	G	A
2002 CANADA	8	8	614		
2003 CANADA	20	20	1659		1a
2004 CANADA	6	5	452		
2005 CANADA	9	8	660		3a
2006 CANADA	15	11	955		3a
2007 CANADA	12	7	709		
2008 CANADA	18	2	645	3g	
2009 CANADA	5	5	392		
2010 CANADA	2	2	72		
2011 CANADA	8	5	376	1g	1a
2012 CANADA	15	5	442		
2013 CANADA	8	4	319	1g	
2014 CANADA	6	1	179		
13 SEASONS	132	83	7474	5g	8a

FIFA / OLYMPIC	MP	MS	MIN	G	A
2003 FIFA WC	6	6	539		1a
2007 FIFA WC	1	0	1		
2008 OLYMPIC	3	0	80		
2011 FIFA WC	2	1	87		
2012 OLYMPIC	3	0	18		

2012 OLYMPIC GAMES • Brittany Timko made three appearances at the London 2012 Olympic Football Tournament when Canada captured an inspiring Bronze Medal. She came off the bench each time in an attacking role and she was part of the attack when Diana Matheson scored her iconic match winner in the last minute against France.

FORWARD

15

LYDIA VAMOS

Born: 1967-08-18, Brantford, ON, CAN. Grew up in Burford, ON, CAN. Height 165 cm.

3 Concacaf medals: Silver in 1991 and 1994, Bronze in 1993
1st #CANWNT: 1990-04-16 at Varna, BUL (v. URS)
1st Goal: 1991-04-16 FWCQ at Port-au-Prince, HAI (v. CRC)

INTERNATIONAL CAREER

Lydia Vamos represented Canada at back-to-back Concacaf Championships in 1991 and 1994, but she missed her chance to go to the FIFA World Cup in 1995 because of an injury.

Vamos was Canada's second-best goal-scorer at the 1991 Concacaf Championship with five goals in five matches, but Canada ultimately missed qualification because only the winners USA advanced to the inaugural FIFA World Cup in 1991.

From 1991 to 1994, Vamos played in 19 straight international matches for Canada, including a third-place finish at the 1993 Concacaf Invitational Tournament. She helped Canada qualify for their first FIFA World Cup by finishing in second place at the 1994 Concacaf Championship.

From 1989 to 1994, Vamos scored seven goals in 24 international "A" matches. She scored another 17 goals in 12 unofficial matches from the 1989 tour to Denmark, the 1990 tour to Bulgaria, two matches against the US "B" team in 1993, and the 1993 World University Games in Hamilton.

CLUB CAREER

Vamos played her club football in Canada and reached Canada Soccer's National Championships four times in a five-year span with either Oakville SC (1989, 1990, 1992) or Scarborough United SC (1993). She won a national silver medal in 1989.

At McMaster University, Vamos led her school to the 1991 CIAU Championship and won the Gunn Baldursson Memorial Award as the tournament's Most Valuable Player.

CANADA RECORDS

"A" RECORDS	MP	MS	MIN	G	A
1989 CANADA	0	0	0		
1990 CANADA	3	1	151		
1991 CANADA	5	4	299	5g	
1993 CANADA	6	6	540	2g	1a
1994 CANADA	10	9	756		
5 SEASONS	**24**	**20**	**1746**	**7g**	**1a**

FIFA / OLYMPIC	MP	MS	MIN	G	A
1995 FIFA WC	INJ	-	-		

● ● ●

1991 CONCACAF CHAMPIONSHIP • Lydia Vamos scored five goals in five matches at the inaugural Concacaf Championship in 1991. She scored in four-straight wins against Costa Rica, Jamaica, Haiti and Trinidad and Tobago (two). Canada finished in second place after they lost to the Americans, who as Concacaf champions qualified for the FIFA World Cup.

MIDFIELDER

19

AMY VERMEULEN

Born: 1983-11-23, Rosetown, SK, CAN. Grew up in Melfort, SK and Saskatoon, SKN. Height 170 cm. Dominant right foot.

1 Concacaf medal: Silver 2006
1st #CANWNT: 2006-08-25 at Rouen, FRA (v. FRA)
1st Goal: 2007-07-18 at Rio, BRA (v. JAM)

INTERNATIONAL CAREER

Amy Vermeulen represented Canada at one FIFA youth tournament and one Pan American Games. She helped Canada win Silver at the inaugural FIFA U-19 World Championship in 2002.

After she made her international "A" debut in 2006, Vermeulen helped Canada finish in second place at the Concacaf Gold Cup. The following year, she helped Canada win a Bronze Medal at the Pan American Games in Brazil.

Vermeulen was 22 years old when she made her international debut on 25 August 2006 in a 1-0 victory over France. She made her last three appearances in 2009 when Canada finished in second place at the Cyprus Cup.

CLUB CAREER

Vermeulen played her club football in Canada and Norway. She reached the USL W-League Final three times: twice with Ottawa Fury FC (2005, 2006) and once with Vancouver Whitecaps FC (2010).

She played her college soccer in the United States at the University of Wisconsin. She was a two-sport star at her school where she also played ice hockey.

Growing up, she played her youth soccer with Saskatoon United. She won a Bronze Medal with Saskatchewan at the 2001 Canada Games in London, Ontario.

CANADA RECORDS

"A" RECORDS	MP	MS	MIN	G	A
2001 CANADA	0	0	0		
2006 CANADA	3	2	176		
2007 CANADA	4	1	115	1g	
2008 CANADA	2	2	107		1a
2009 CANADA	3	0	51		
5 SEASONS	**12**	**5**	**449**	**1g**	**1a**

PAN AMERICAN GAMES • Amy Vermeulen made four appearances at the 2007 Pan American Games in Rio de Janeiro when Canada won a Bronze Medal. She scored her first career international goal in the group phase against Jamaica when Canada won 11-1 at the Zico Football Centre (she scored the 6-0 goal in the first half).

FORWARD

13

EVELYNE VIENS

Born: 1997-02-06, L'Ancienne-Lorette, QC, CAN. Height 173 cm. Dominant right foot.

1 Olympic Games: Gold at Tokyo in 2021
1 FIFA World Cup: AU NZ 2023
1st #CANWNT: 2021-02-18 at Orlando, FL, USA (v. USA)
1st Goal: 2021-04-09 at Cardiff, WAL (v. WAL)

OLYMPIC CHAMPION

Evelyne Viens has already represented Canada at one Olympic Games and one FIFA World Cup with Canada. She won an Olympic Gold Medal in 2021.

Viens made her debut with Canada just five months before the Olympic Games at the 2021 SheBelieves Cup in Orlando, Florida. That year, she helped Canada set a program record with a 12-match undefeated streak.

In 2023, she made her FIFA World Cup debut in Australia in the tournament opener against Nigeria.

AS ROMA

Viens joined AS Roma in Italy ahead of the 2023-24 season. She scored three goals in UEFA club competitions.

In Sweden in 2022, Viens set the league record for most goals by a Canadian player. With 21 goals in 26 matches, she ranked second in the league scoring race behind only Linköping's Amalie Vangsgaard (22

goals). In 2023 before her move to Italy, she scored 12 goals in 17 matches.

Before moving to Sweden, Viens played her pro football in USA and France. She made her professional debut on 30 June 2020.

In Canada, she won back-to-back CCAA Championships and was the nation's Player of the Year in 2015. She then played college soccer at the University of South Florida in the United States.

CANADA RECORDS

"A" RECORDS	MP	MS	MIN	G	A
2021 CANADA	10	2	362	2g	
2022 CANADA	4	2	214	1g	1a
2023 CANADA	8	3	262	1g	
FIRST 2 YEARS	**22**	**7**	**838**	**4g**	**1a**

FIFA / OLYMPIC	MP	MS	MIN	G	A
2021 OLYMPIC	2	1	61		
2023 FIFA WC	3	1	97		

● ● ●

1st INTERNATIONAL GOAL • Evelyne Viens scored her first two international goals in the build up to the 2021 Olympic Football Tournament. She scored her first goal in a 3-0 away victory over Wales from inside the six-yard box, then scored the match winner four days later in a 2-0 away victory over England.

13

MIDFIELDER

AMY WALSH

Born: 1977-09-13, Montréal, QC, CAN. Grew up in St-Bruno, QC, CAN. Height 177 cm. Dominant right foot.

2 FIFA World Cups: Group phase at USA 1999 and China 2007
1 Olympic Games: Quarterfinals at Beijing 2008
4 Concacaf medals: Gold 1998, Silver 2002, 2006, 2008
1st #CANWNT: 1998-07-19 at Ottawa, ON, CAN (v. CHN)
1st Goal: 2000-03-16 at Albufeira, POR (v. FIN)

CANADA SOCCER HALL OF FAME

Amy Walsh represented Canada at two FIFA World Cups and one Olympic Games. She won the 1998 Concacaf Championship and she won a Bronze Medal at the 2007 Pan American Games.

She made 102 international appearances for Canada across 12 years and she wore the captain's armband more than 30 times.

She led Canada in minutes played in both 1999 and 2000 and she set a record by making 43 consecutive appearances for Canada from 1998 to 2001.

In her Olympic debut against Sweden in 2008, she recorded an assist on Melissa Tancredi's goal in the second half.

Walsh made her Canada debut on 19 July 1998 in a 2-1 loss to China PR in Ottawa. Both Amy and her sister Cindy made their debuts in the same match. Two years later, Amy scored her first international goal in a 2-1 win over Finland at the 2000 Algarve Cup.

She played her club football in Canada and the United States. As a pro rookie, she helped the Atlanta Beat reach the 2001 WUSA Final. In Canada, she reached the 2003 National Championships Final with FC Sélect Rive-Sud. As a youth player, she won the U-19 Cup in 1996 with Lakeshore SC.

CANADA RECORDS

"A" RECORDS	MP	MS	MIN	G	A
1998 CANADA	8	8	675		
1999 CANADA	11	11	990		
2000 CANADA	18	18	1615	4g	1a
2001 CANADA	10	10	822		1a
2002 CANADA	9	6	589	1g	1a
2003 CANADA	0	0	0		
2005 CANADA	10	10	849		1a
2006 CANADA	16	16	1378		
2007 CANADA	8	5	459		1a
2008 CANADA	8	2	284		1a
2009 CANADA	4	1	101		
11 SEASONS	**102**	**87**	**7762**	**5g**	**6a**

FIFA / OLYMPIC	MP	MS	MIN	G	A
1999 FIFA WC	3	3	270		
2007 FIFA WC	1	0	17		
2008 OLYMPIC	1	0	45		1a

1999 FIFA WORLD CUP • Amy Walsh featured in every Canada minute across the 1999 international season, including all three matches at the FIFA Women's World Cup in the United States. She was one of nine players on the Canada squad that featured in every minute against Japan, Norway and Russia through the group phase.

CENTRE BACK

CINDY WALSH

Born: 1979-09-13, Montréal, QC, CAN. Grew up in St-Bruno, QC, CAN. Height 168 cm. Dominant right foot.

1 Concacaf medal: Gold in 1998
1st #CANWNT: 1998-07-19 at Ottawa, ON, CAN (v. CHN)

CONCACAF CHAMPION

Cindy Walsh helped Canada win the 1998 Concacaf Championship and then finish in fourth place at the 2000 Concacaf Gold Cup. She also helped Canada's youth team finish in fourth place at the Pan American Games in 1999.

Walsh made her international debut in a 2-1 loss to China in Ottawa (older sister Amy was a starter while Cindy was a late substitute). Less than six weeks later, Cindy was one of two teenagers selected to the Canada squad for the 1998 Concacaf Championship in Toronto (alongside Karina LeBlanc).

Walsh played 20 times for Canada from 1998 to 2000, in fact every time with her older sister Amy also in the lineup.

Ten years after her last match with Head Coach Even Pellerud in 2000, Cindy Walsh returned to the Canada lineup with new Head Coach Carolina Morace at the 2010 Cyprus Cup. She played in a friendly and three group matches before Canada won the March tournament with a 1-0 win over New Zealand in the 2010 Final.

CLUB CAREER

Walsh played her club and college soccer in Canada and the United States. In 2013 as player-coach of the Comètes de Laval, she reached the USL W-League Championship Final.

She played college soccer at the University of Hartford where she was the America East Rookie of the Year in 2000.

At the youth level, she was a national runner up with AS Brossard at Canada Soccer's U-17 Cup in 1994.

CANADA RECORDS

"A" RECORDS	MP	MS	MIN	G	A
1998 CANADA	4	1	127		
1999 CANADA	2	1	91		
2000 CANADA	14	14	1191		
2010 CANADA	4	1	145		
4 SEASONS	**24**	**17**	**1554**		

● ● ●

1998 CONCACAF CHAMPIONSHIP • Cindy Walsh was just 18 years old when she won a Concacaf title with Canada in 1998. She made one appearance in that tournament as a substitute against Puerto Rico. Two years later, she made three appearances at the 2000 Concacaf Gold Cup when Canada finished in fourth place.

7 RHIAN WILKINSON

RIGHT BACK / F

Born: 1982-05-12, Pointe-Claire, QC, CAN. Grew up in Baie d'Urfé, QC, CAN. Height 166 cm. Dominant right foot.

4 FIFA World Cups: 2003, 2007, 2011, 2015
3 Olympic Games: Quarterfinals 2008, Bronze 2012 and 2016
6 Concacaf: Gold 2010, Silver 2006, 2008, 2012, 2016, Bronze '04
1st #CANWNT: 2003-04-26 at Washington, DC, USA (v. USA)
1st Goal: 2003-07-17 at Montréal, QC, CAN (v. BRA)

CANADA SOCCER HALL OF FAME

Rhian Wilkinson won two Bronze Medals from three Olympic Games, featured in four FIFA World Cups, and won a Concacaf Championship as an international footballer with Canada. When she left the game, she ranked third all time with 181 appearances.

She played every match across her first three FIFA World Cups including a fourth-place finish at USA 2003. She also played in every Canada match at the 2008 and 2012 Olympic Games.

In 2006, she scored in the victory that qualified Canada to the 2007 FIFA World Cup in China.

At the club level, Wilkinson played her football in Canada, USA and Norway. She made one appearance in UEFA Champions League Qualifying with Team Strømmen (later known as Lillestrøm SK). In 2012, she won the Toppserien title with Lillestrøm SK.

She played in two USL W-League Finals with the Ottawa Fury (2005, 2006).

CANADA RECORDS

"A" RECORDS		MP	MS	MIN	G	A
2003	CANADA	12	2	408	3g	
2004	CANADA	4	1	141		
2005	CANADA	2	2	169		
2006	CANADA	14	12	1070	2g	2a
2007	CANADA	13	10	921	2g	1a
2008	CANADA	22	22	2016		4a
2009	CANADA	5	5	448		1a
2010	CANADA	16	15	1325		3a
2011	CANADA	22	20	1811		
2012	CANADA	21	18	1556		6a
2013	CANADA	15	12	982		1a
2014	CANADA	10	10	819		2a
2015	CANADA	12	11	894		2a
2016	CANADA	12	10	758		
2017	CANADA	1	0	33		
15 SEASONS		**181**	**150**	**13,351**	**7g**	**22a**

FIFA / OLYMPIC	MP	MS	MIN	G	A
2003 FIFA WC	6	1	159		
2007 FIFA WC	3	1	162		
2008 OLYMPIC	4	4	390		1a
2011 FIFA WC	3	3	270		
2012 OLYMPIC	6	6	551		2a
2015 FIFA WC	3	2	159		
2016 OLYMPIC	3	3	196		

2012 OLYMPIC GAMES • Right back Rhian Wilkinson featured in all six Canada matches when they won a memorable Bronze Medal at the Olympic Football Tournament in 2012. In the group phase, she got assists on two goals scored by Melissa Tancredi: Canada's first goal of the tournament (a 2-1 loss to Japan) and their first goal against Sweden (a 2-2 draw).

CENTRE BACK

20

SHANNON WOELLER

Born: 1990-01-31, Vancouver, BC, CAN.   Height 172 cm.
Dominent left foot.

1 FIFA World Cup: Round of 16 at France 2019
1 Concacaf medal: Silver in 2012
1st #CANWNT: 2009-03-07 at Larnaka, CYP (v. NED)

INTERNATIONAL CAREER

Shannon Woeller has represented Canada at one FIFA youth tournament and one FIFA World Cup. She won a Concacaf youth title in 2008 and the Pan American Games Gold Medal in 2011.

In December 2010, she helped Canada win the Torneio Internacional in Brazil, which was part of an 11-match undefeated streak (a new program record). In January 2012, she won a Concacaf Silver Medal when Canada qualified for the Olympic Games.

After she missed the Olympic cut in July 2012, and then had some set backs through injuries at the club level, she worked her way back into the Canada squad in April 2017 and earned a selection to the FIFA World Cup team in 2019.

VITTSJÖ GIK HÄSSLEHOLM

Woeller has played her club football in Canada, Norway, Iceland, Germany, Sweden and Spain. She joined Vittsjö GIK Hässleholm ahead of the 2024 season in Sweden.

Woeller has finished as high as fourth in the Damallsvenskan standings with Eskilstuna United in 2019. When she played in Iceland, she reached the UEFA Champions League Round of 32 with UMF Stjarnan.

After recovering from a 2016 knee injury, Woeller moved to Germany where she made her Bundesliga debut in February 2017 with FF USV Jena. In 2017-18, she became the first Canadian to feature in all 22 league matches in the Bundesliga.

CANADA RECORDS

"A" RECORDS	MP	MS	MIN	G	A
2009 CANADA	2	0	50		
2010 CANADA	2	1	104		
2011 CANADA	5	5	480		
2012 CANADA	7	6	572		1a
2017 CANADA	2	0	21		
2018 CANADA	1	0	37		
2019 CANADA	2	1	46		
FIRST 11 YEARS	21	13	1310		1a

FIFA / OLYMPIC	MP	MS	MIN	G	A
2019 FIFA WC	0	0	0		

● ● ●

2011 PAN AMERICAN GAMES • Centre back Shannon Woeller featured in every minute when Canada captured a Gold Medal at the Pan American Games Guadalajara 2011 with new Head Coach John Herdman. In the group phase, Woeller earned Player of the Match honours in Canada's 1-0 victory over Argentina.

GOALKEEPER

NICCI WRIGHT

Born: 1972-08-12, Nicole Wright. Grew up in Duncan, BC, CAN. Height 180 cm. Dominant right foot.

1 FIFA World Cup: Group phase at USA 1999
1 Concacaf medal: Gold in 1998
1st #CANWNT: 1996-05-15 at New Britain, CT, USA (v. CHN)
1st Clean Sheet: 1998-08-28 FWCQ at Toronto, ON, CAN (v. PUR)

CONCACAF CHAMPION

Nicci Wright represented Canada at the 1999 FIFA World Cup after winning the Concacaf Championship in 1998. She also played for Canada when they finished in fourth place at the inaugural Concacaf Gold Cup in 2000.

With Canada from 1996 to 2002, Wright made 37 international "A" appearances, at the time a record for Canadian goalkeepers. She also played in 16 consecutive matches from 1996 to 1999, a Canadian goalkeeper record that still stands more than 20 years later.

She was 23 years old when she made her international "A" debut on 15 May 1996 in a 5-0 loss to China. She later posted five-straight clean sheets at the 1998 Concacaf Championship and featured in all three group matches at the 1999 FIFA World Cup.

CLUB CAREER

Wright played her club football in Canada and the United States, notably helping the Washington Freedom win the 2003 WUSA Founders Cup. Two years earlier, she helped the Vancouver Breakers reach the USL W-League Final.

Wright also played soccer at the University of Victoria. At the youth level, she helped British Columbia win the first Canada Games Gold Medal in 1993.

After her career, she was honoured by the University of Victoria Sports Hall of Fame in 2013 and the Canada West Hall of Fame in 2019.

CANADA RECORDS

"A" RECORDS		MP	MS	MIN		CS
1996	CANADA	3	3	270	0	CS
1997	CANADA	3	3	280	0	CS
1998	CANADA	8	8	675	5	CS
1999	CANADA	8	8	720	2	CS
2000	CANADA	9	9	840	2	CS
2001	CANADA	5	5	405	1	CS
2002	CANADA	1	1	90	1	CS
7 SEASONS		37	37	3280	11	CS

FIFA / OLYMPIC		MP	MS	MIN		CS
1999	FIFA WC	3	3	270	0	CS

1998 CONCACAF WOMEN'S CHAMPIONSHIP • Nicci Wright posted five-straight clean sheets at the 1998 Concacaf Championship when Canada won their first confederation title in women's football. In the knockout phase, Canada beat Costa Rica in the Semifinals (2-0) and Mexico in the Concacaf Final (1-0).

CENTRE BACK

SHELINA ZADORSKY

Born: 1992-10-24, London, ON, CAN. Grew up in Kitchener & London, ON, CAN. Height 173 cm. Dominant left foot.

2 FIFA World Cups: France 2019, AU NZ 2023
2 Olympic Games: Bronze at Rio 2016, Gold at Tokyo in 2021
4 Concacaf medals: Silver 2016, 2018, 2020, 2022
1st #CANWNT: 2013-01-14 at Yongchuan, CHN (v. KOR)
1st Goal: 2016-03-09 at Faro, POR (v. BRA)

OLYMPIC CHAMPION

Shelina Zadorsky has already represented Canada at two FIFA youth tournaments, two FIFA World Cups and two Olympic Games. In 2021, she helped Canada set a program record with a 12-match undefeated streak.

She won an Olympic Bronze Medal at Rio 2016 and an Olympic Gold Medal at Tokyo in 2021.

In 2016, she scored her first international goal when Canada won their first Algarve Cup title against Brazil. In 2017, she was Canada's leader in minutes played.

At the 2019 FIFA World Cup, she played in every Canada minute when they reached the Round of 16.

TOTTENHAM HOTSPUR FC

Zadorsky joined Tottenham Hotspur FC ahead of the 2020-21 season in England's FA Women's Super League. She helped the club finish third in the league standings in 2021-22. She was the team's Player of the Season in 2020-21.

Zadorsky previously played her football in Canada, Sweden, Australia and USA. In 2014, she helped the Perth Glory win the W-League Premiership. In 2016, she helped the Washington Spirit reach the NWSL Final in the playoffs.

CANADA RECORDS

"A" RECORDS		MP	MS	MIN	G	A
2012	CANADA	0	0	0		
2013	CANADA	1	1	63		
2015	CANADA	3	1	85		
2016	CANADA	18	18	1485	1g	
2017	CANADA	12	12	1080		
2018	CANADA	11	9	844		1a
2019	CANADA	14	14	1215		
2020	CANADA	7	7	630	1g	2a
2021	CANADA	11	9	811		
2022	CANADA	10	9	810	2g	
2023	CANADA	8	2	357		
FIRST 12 YEARS		**95**	**82**	**7380**	**4g**	**3a**

FIFA / OLYMPIC		MP	MS	MIN	G	A
2016	OLYMPIC	5	5	379		
2019	FIFA WC	4	4	360		
2021	OLYMPIC	3	2	181		
2023	FIFA WC	1	0	45		

● ● ●

2021 OLYMPIC GAMES • Shelina Zadorsky has already made eight Olympic appearances including the full 90 minutes when Canada beat Brazil for a Bronze Medal at the 2016 Olympic Games in Brazil. She made her 75th career appearance when Canada won their Gold Medal at the 2021 Olympic Football Tournament in Tokyo.

2

EMILY ZURRER

CENTRE BACK

Born: 1987-07-12, Vancouver, BC, CAN. Grew up in Crofton, BC, CAN. Height 178 cm. Dominant left foot.

2 FIFA World Cups: Group phase 2011, Quarterfinals 2015
2 Olympic Games: Quarterfinals in 2008, Bronze in 2012
1 Concacaf medal: Gold in 2010
1st #CANWNT: 2004-07-03 at Nashville, TN, USA (v. USA)
1st Goal: 2011-03-02 at Larnaka, CYP (v. SCO)

OLYMPIC BRONZE MEDAL

Emily Zurrer represented Canada at two FIFA youth tournaments, two FIFA World Cups and two Olympic Games. She won MVP honours at the Concacaf Under-19 Championship in 2004 when Canada lifted the U-19 title.

She won an Olympic Bronze Medal with Canada in 2012, although she didn't get to see action after she was injured just before the tournament.

From late 2010 to early 2011, she helped Canada set a program record with an 11-match undefeated streak. Inside that streak, she helped Canada win the 2010 Concacaf Championship.

After the streak, she scored Canada's series-winning goal in the 2011 Cyprus Cup Final. She scored the 2-1 winner against the Netherlands in extra time.

From 2004 to 2015, Zurrer made 82 career international appearances with Canada. She was just 16 years old when she made her debut in a 1-0 loss to the United States on 3 July 2004.

CLUB CAREER

Zurrer played her club football in Canada, USA, Germany and Sweden. She helped Vancouver Whitecaps FC win the 2006 USL W-League Championship and then reach the Final once again in 2010.

She was honoured by the Soccer Hall of Fame of British Columbia in 2021.

CANADA RECORDS

"A" RECORDS	MP	MS	MIN	G	A
2004 CANADA	2	2	180		
2008 CANADA	12	11	1009		
2009 CANADA	6	6	540		
2010 CANADA	12	12	1052		
2011 CANADA	18	16	1560	2g	3a
2012 CANADA	5	4	315	1g	
2013 CANADA	15	7	705		
2014 CANADA	8	6	514		
2015 CANADA	4	1	209		
9 SEASONS	82	65	6084	3g	3a

FIFA / OLYMPIC	MP	MS	MIN	G	A
2008 OLYMPIC	4	4	381		
2011 FIFA WC	3	3	270		
2012 OLYMPIC	INJ	0	0		
2015 FIFA WC	0	0	0		

2008 OLYMPIC GAMES • Emily Zurrer featured in all four Canada matches at the 2008 Olympic Football Tournament when they reached the Quarterfinals before the Americans won in extra time. Four years later, she was selected to the Canada squad for the London 2012 Olympic Games, but she missed the tournament through injury.

MIDFIELDER

MARIE-YASMINE ALIDOU

Born: 1995-04-28, Montréal, QC, CAN. Grew up in Saint-Hubert, QC, CAN. Height 160 cm. Dominant right foot.
1st #CANWNT: 2022-02-23 at Wolverhampton, ENG (v. Spain)

Marie-Yasmine Alidou came up through Canada Soccer's National Training Centre program, but did not feature with Canada's youth teams. She has since played in France, Sweden, Spain, Norway and Portugal. She won the Taça de Portugal with FC Famalicão in 2023.

WINGER

AMANDA ALLEN

Born: 2005-02-21, Mississauga, ON, CAN. Height 163 cm. Dominant right foot.
1st #CANWNT: 2022-11-11 at Santos, BRA (v. Brazil)

After representing Canada at the 2022 FIFA U-17 World Cup, Amanda Allen helped Canada qualify for the 2024 FIFA U-20 World Cup in June 2023. Allen made her professional debut in May 2023 with Orlando Pride in the National Women's Soccer League.

MIDFIELDER

SIMI AWUJO

Born: 2003-09-23, Atlanta, GA, USA. Height 175 cm. Dominant right foot.
1st #CANWNT: 2022-09-23 at Brisbane, AUS (v. Australia)

After representing Canada at the 2022 FIFA U-20 World Cup in Costa Rica, Simi Awujo made her full National Team debut with Canada the following month in Australia. She was Canada Soccer's 2022 Young Player of the Year.

FORWARD

TANYA BOYCHUK

Born: 2000-06-20, Edmonton, AB, CAN. Height 170 cm. Dominant right foot. Got her first #CANWNT call up from coach Bev Priestman in February 2022.

Tanya Boychuk represented Canada at two Concacaf Under-20 Championships before she got her first call up to the full National Team. A Canada Games tournament all-star in 2017, she has played her college soccer at the University of Memphis.

ZOE BURNS

MIDFIELDER

Born: 2002-01-05, Puyallup, WA, USA. Grew up in Issaquah, WA, USA. Height 158 cm. Dominant right foot.
1st #CANWNT: 2022-04-11 at Langford, BC, CAN (v. Nigeria)

Zoe Burns helped Canada qualify for the 2023 FIFA World Cup and then finish in second place at the 2022 Concacaf W Championship in July. The following month, she represented Canada at the FIFA U-20 World Cup in Costa Rica.

ASHLEY CATHRO

FULLBACK

Born: 2000-01-19, Victoria, BC, CAN. Height 170 cm. Dominant left foot. Got her first #CANWNT call up from coach John Herdman in January 2017.

The BC Soccer Youth Player of the Year in 2015-16, Ashley Cathro represented Canada at the FIFA U-17 World Cup in 2016. She has played her college soccer at the University of Illinois and earned her first call up with coach Bev Priestman in November 2021.

SAMANTHA CHANG

MIDFIELDER

Born: 2000-07-13, Mississauga, ON, CAN. Height 165 cm. Dominant right foot.
1st #CANWNT: 2021-02-21 at Orlando, FL, USA (v. Argentina)

Samantha Chang helped Canada win the 2014 Concacaf Girls' Under-15 Championship and two years later participate at the FIFA U-17 World Cup in Jordan. After playing her college soccer at the University of South Carolina, she turned pro with SCU Torreense in Portugal.

ANNABELLE CHUKWU

FORWARD

Born: 2007-02-08, London, ENG. Grew up in Ottawa, ON, CAN. Height 168 cm. Dominant right foot. Got her first #CANWNT call up from coach Bev Priestman in November 2022.

After representing Canada at the 2022 FIFA U-17 World Cup, Annabelle Chukwu helped Canada qualify for the 2024 FIFA U-20 World Cup in June 2023. She co-led Canada with four goals at the 2023 Concacaf Under-20 Championship.

CENTRE BACK

SYDNEY COLLINS

Born: 1999-09-08, Hillsboro, OR, USA. Grew up in Beaverton, OR, USA. Height 173 cm. Dominant right foot. Got her first #CANWNT call up from coach Bev Priestman in February 2023.

After representing the United States at the youth level, Sydney Collins has come into Canada Soccer's Women's National Team with coach Priestman. She turned pro in 2023 with North Carolina Courage in the National Women's Soccer League.

FORWARD

JESSICA DE FILIPPO

Born: 2001-04-20, Mississauga, ON, CAN. Grew up in Montréal, QC, CAN. Height 174 cm. Dominant right foot. Got her first #CANWNT call up from coach Kenneth Heiner-Møller in October 2019.

Jessica De Filippo represented Canada at the FIFA U-17 World Cup in 2018 and then played her college soccer at the University of Arkansas. She turned pro in February 2023 with 1. FFC Turbine Potsdam in the German Bundesliga.

GOALKEEPER

ANNA KARPENKO

Born: 2002-04-10, Toronto, ON, CAN. Grew up in Richmond Hill, ON, CAN. Height 173 cm. Got her first #CANWNT call up from coach Bev Priestman in November 2021.

Anna Karpenko represented Canada at two FIFA youth tournaments and she won a Golden Glove Award at the 2022 Concacaf Under-20 Championship. She has played her college soccer at Harvard University in the United States.

FORWARD

CLARISSA LARISEY

Born: 1999-07-02, Ottawa, ON, CAN. Height 172 cm. Dominant right foot.
1st #CANWNT: 2022-09-03 at Brisbane, AUS (v. Australia)

Clarissa Larisey has played her club football in Iceland, Scotland and Sweden since turning pro in 2021. She won the league title with Valur in Iceland and then won both the Scottish Cup and Scottish League Cup with Glasgow's Celtic FC.

MARIE LEVASSEUR

FULLBACK

Born: 1997-05-18, Stoneham, QC, CAN. Height 172 cm. Dominant right foot.
1st #CANWNT: 2015-12-13 at Natal, BRA (v. Trinidad and Tobago)

Marie Levasseur represented Canada at two FIFA youth tournaments before turning pro in Finland with ONS Oulu. She has since played her club football in France and will play for Montpellier HSC in 2023-24.

JORDYN LISTRO

MIDFIELDER

Born: 1995-08-10, Toronto, ON, CAN. Height 165 cm. Dominant right foot.
1st #CANWNT: 2021-02-21 at Orlando, FL, USA (v. Argentina)

Jordyn Listro represented Canada at the FIFA U-17 World Cup in Azerbaijan before playing her college soccer at the University of South Florida. After briefly playing pro football in Spain, she joined the National Women's Soccer League ranks in 2020.

ELLA OTTEY

LEFT BACK

Born: 2005-08-12, Toronto, ON, CAN. Height 170 cm. Dominant left foot. Got her first #CANWNT call up from coach Bev Priestman in November 2022.

After representing Canada at the 2022 FIFA U-17 World Cup, Ella Ottey helped Canada qualify for the 2024 FIFA U-20 World Cup in June 2023. She scored a goal and got two assists in that match that qualified Canada for the FIFA tournament.

VICTORIA PICKETT

MIDFIELDER

Born: 1996-08-12, Newmarket, ON, CAN. Grew up in Barrie, ON, CAN. Height 167 cm. Dominant right foot.
1st #CANWNT: 2021-11-27 at Ciudad México, DF, MEX (v. Mexico)

Victoria Pickett represented Canada at three FIFA youth tournaments before turning pro in April 2021 with Kansas City in the National Women's Soccer League. After being traded to NJ/NY Gotham FC in 2022, she was traded to North Carolina Courage in April 2023.

LYSIANNE PROULX

GOALKEEPER

Born: 1999-04-17, Longueuil, QC, CAN. Grew up in Boucherville, QC, CAN. Height 173 cm. Dominant right foot. Got her first #CANWNT call up from coach Bev Priestman in June 2022.

After winning the Concacaf Girls' Under-15 Championship in 2014, Lysianne Proulx went on to represent Canada at three FIFA youth tournaments. She turned pro at the start of the 2022-23 season with SCU Torreense in Portugal.

JADE ROSE

CENTRE BACK

Born: 2003-02-12, Markham, ON, CAN. Height 178 cm. Dominant right foot.
1st #CANWNT: 2021-02-21 at Orlando, FL, USA (v. Argentina)

Jade Rose represented Canada at two FIFA youth tournaments and she won Canada Soccer's Young Player of the Year Award in both 2020 and 2021. She has played her college soccer at Harvard University in the United States.

BIANCA ST-GEORGES

RIGHT BACK

Born: 1997-07-28, St-Charles-Borommée, QC, CAN. Height 167 cm. Dominant right foot.
1st #CANWNT: 2021-06-11 at Cartagena, ESP (v. Czech Republic)

Bianca St-Georges represented Canada at two FIFA youth tournaments and was the team captain at the FIFA U-20 World Cup in 2016. After she missed her first pro season through injury, she was the Chicago Red Stars' Rookie of the Year in 2021.

NIKAYLA SMALL

MIDFIELDER

Born: 2003-03-24, Toronto, ON, CAN. Grew up in Pickering, ON, CAN. Height 155 cm. Dominant right foot. Got her first #CANWNT call up from coach Bev Priestman in October 2021.

After she earned her first two call ups to the National Team in 2021, Nikayla Small represented Canada at the FIFA U-20 World Cup in 2022. She has played her college soccer at Wake Forest University in the United State.

OLIVIA SMITH

FORWARD

Born: 2004-08-05, North York, ON, CAN. Grew up in Whitby, ON, CAN. Height 160 cm. Dominant right foot.
1st #CANWNT: 2019-11-07 at Yongchuan, CHN (v. Brazil)

After representing Canada at the 2022 FIFA U-20 World Cup, Olivia Smith helped Canada qualify for the 2024 FIFA U-20 World Cup in June 2023. She co-led Canada with four goals at the 2023 Concacaf Under-20 Championship.

SARAH STRATIGAKIS

MIDFIELDER

Born: 1999-03-07, Scarborough, ON, CAN. Grew up in Woodbridge, ON, CAN. Height 161 cm. Dominant right foot.
1st #CANWNT: 2017-02-04 at Vancouver, BC, CAN (v. Mexico)

After winning the Concacaf Girls' Under-15 Championship in 2014, Sarah Stratigakis went on to represent Canada at three FIFA youth tournaments. She turned pro in 2022 with Vittsjö GIK in the Swedish Damallsvenskan.

AMANDA WEST

FORWARD

Born: 2001-02-11, Sundsvall, SWE. Grew up in Burlington, ON, CAN. Height 165 cm. Dominant right foot. Got her first #CANWNT call up from coach Bev Priestman in November 2021.

As a youth player, Amanda West won silver and bronze medals at Canada Soccer's U-17 Cup with Burlington YSC in 2017 and 2018. She has played her college soccer at the University of Pittsburgh in the United States.

SURA YEKKA

RIGHT BACK

Born: 1997-01-04, Toronto, ON, CAN. Grew up in Mississauga, ON, CAN. Height 165 cm. Dominant right foot.
1st #CANWNT: 2013-10-30 at Edmonton, AB, CAN (v. Korea Republic)

Canada Soccer's U-17 Player of the Year in 2013, Sura Yekka represented Canada at three FIFA youth tournaments from 2014 to 2016. Since turning pro in 2020, she has played her club football in Germany, France and Sweden.

BOOKS BY UP NORTH PRODUCTIONS

Canada from Bronze to Gold
(Women's National Team 2010-2021)

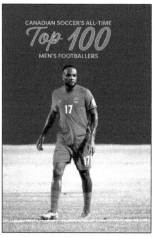

Canadian Soccer's All-Time
Top 100 Men's Footballers

Canadian Soccer's 2024 Men's
Football Annual

SOCCER FOOTBALL BOOKS :

CANADA FROM BRONZE TO GOLD
CHRISTINE SINCLAIR THE G.O.A.T. - 12 FAMOUS MATCHES FOR CANADA
CANADIAN SOCCER'S ALL-TIME TOP 100 WOMEN'S FOOTBALLERS
CANADIAN SOCCER'S ALL-TIME TOP 100 MEN'S FOOTBALLERS
CANADIAN SOCCER'S 2024 MEN'S FOOTBALL ANNUAL
THIS DAY IN CANADIAN SOCCER HISTORY
CANADIAN SOCCER HISTORY: MEN'S AMATEUR FOOTBALL CHAMPIONS
26 REMARKABLE MOMENTS IN CANADIAN SOCCER HISTORY

HOCKEY BOOKS :

THE WAYNE GRETZKY GOALS RECORD
12 SEASONS: THE CWHL RECORDS BOOK
WHO'S WHO IN WOMEN'S HOCKEY GUIDE
GAME 7 : RECORDS, HEROES & CHAMPIONS

COLLECTOR BOOKS :

THE O-PEE-CHEE HOCKEY CARD STORY
1979-80 O-PEE-CHEE HOCKEY CARD STORY
THE PARKIES HOCKEY CARD STORY
THE O-PEE-CHEE MASTER CHECKLIST
THE O-PEE-CHEE HOCKEY CARD MASTER CHECKLIST
100 HOCKEY CARD FIRSTS
COLLECTING THE TOP 100: MONTRÉAL CANADIENS
COLLECTING THE TOP 100: TORONTO MAPLE LEAFS
COLLECTING THE TOP 100: O-PEE-CHEE HOCKEY CARDS
THE WAYNE GRETZKY COLLECTOR'S HANDBOOK
THE EXPOS BASEBALL CARD MASTER CHECKLIST